MEMOIRS OF A PUBLIC BABY

MEMOIRS OF
A PUBLIC BABY

by

PHILIP O'CONNOR

With a New Introduction

by

STEPHEN SPENDER

W. W. NORTON & COMPANY
New York   London

Copyright © 1988, 1958 by Philip O'Connor
Introduction to Second Edition © 1988 by Stephen Spender
First American Edition, 1989.

Printed in the United States of America.

Library of Congress Cataloging-in-Publication Data

O'Connor, Philip.
    Memoirs of a public baby/by Philip O'Connor; with a new introduction by
    Stephen Spender.
        p.   cm.
    1. O'Connor, Philip—Biography. 2. Poets, English—20th century—
    Biography.   I. Title.
    PR6029.C62Z467   1988
    821'.914—dc19
    [B]   89-3250

ISBN 0-393-02763-5

W. W. Norton & Company, Inc., 500 Fifth Avenue, New York, N.Y. 10110
W. W. Norton & Company Ltd., 37 Great Russell Street, London WC1B 3NU

1 2 3 4 5 6 7 8 9 0

For

EDITH   YOUNG

CONTENTS

INTRODUCTION TO SECOND EDITION
by STEPHEN SPENDER
page 7

INTRODUCTION TO FIRST EDITION
page 13

PART ONE: PREMATURITY
page 19

PART TWO: WAITING FOR THE END
page 149

PART THREE: THE END THAT FAILED
page 211

NOTE

I wish to express my gratitude to the Hon. Simon Stuart for his patient and hard work of imposing a chronological order, deleting repetitions and generally editing an extremely untidy narrative.

P. O'C.

The grandeur of the soul does not consist in flying high, but in walking orderly; its grandeur does not exercise in grandeur, but in mediocrity.

MONTAIGNE

INTRODUCTION
TO SECOND EDITION
By STEPHEN SPENDER

Re-reading Philip O'Connor's memoirs of his Childhood, Boyhood and Youth thirty years after I first wrote an Introduction to them, it strikes me that I forgot to mention that this is a Chaplinesque comic masterpiece. What O'Connor writes about Chaplin illuminates his own work and character:

> More directly and vividly than any other, he justified my ways because he showed how sensible, logical behaviour led to confusion, how simple people get into a mess and how scoundrels have the best haircuts and incomes. I intuitively disagreed that the sensible straightforward actions such as Chaplin's should be 'funny', whereas crooked complex ones, such as the morons' in other American films should be 'sensible'.

O'Connor here identifies with Chaplin as the sensible, logical person. This identification also projects the opposite of Chaplin/O'Connor's world of complex and crooked morons. The O'Connor – or Chaplinesque – world implies the existence of another alien world; and the two worlds having nothing in common are completely opposite. There is an 'I' who is Chaplin/O'Connor and there is a 'They' of the morons. Chaplin/O'Connor can never say 'we' in the sense of including the moronic 'They' as a shared consciousness: though the Chaplin/

7

O'Connor 'I' might find some waif, some blind or beggar girl whom it could absorb within its world as a fellow victim of the world of morons.

Characteristically, at school O'Connor together with his 'lieutenant, Allen' takes over, as the one fellow pupil with whom he can have any contact, a 'boy with the unbelievable name of Donald Darling, who appeared to me to have the unpleasant aspect of combined milk and urine in his face'. O'Connor happens according to his own account to have been cruel to Donald Darling, but he might equally have overwhelmed him with kindness. He also has his 'ally' Allen: but such an ally is a satellite, he is not an equal. The other children representing the outside, moronic population are automata:

> The children were almost little institutions, little snippets of ideology. Their moral 'Oooo's' and 'Aaah's' made me groan, their legalistic little minds, which sped them off to tell some wretched authority about every mishap, their dingy volubility about what was fair and what wasn't, their shouting declarations of their 'rights' – all these things, like civilization itself, depressed me.

For each one of us there is, of course, a gap between inner worlds of the 'I' and outer worlds of the 'They': but for most of us outer and inner are connected by a bridge of 'we' – family, class, education, shared values. One can scarcely imagine Philip O'Connor using the pronoun 'we' in this sense. His world is most decidedly a world of alienation. He is *not* alienated only during that part of his childhood spent in Wimereux with the Tillieux family. But the sense of 'belonging' that he felt when he was sharing a bed with Madame was more that of returning to the womb than that of being one member of the family or community.

As he gets older O'Connor becomes aware of himself as alienated. He attributes this partly to his upbringing with its effects on his psychology, and partly to the class system – a semi-Marxist self-analysis. During a short period in which he attended meetings of a communist group in Wimbledon, he comes, in his description of this, nearest to thinking that he might belong to some kind of proletarian 'us'. He writes of the members of this group or cell almost with awe and a sense of in-other-circumstances-perhaps-belonging which he feels about no other group, although at the same time he is certain that he cannot belong to it:

> I gained a strong impression of this sample of the 'working-class mind' – mine was already of the splenetic lower-middle kind. Their slowness was beyond my belief, forcing me impatiently into spectacular errors . . . Nevertheless, the actual progress of their physiognomically demonstrated understanding was as good as a good sunrise, as good as intelligent children with the extra undertones of emotional understanding and experience . . . Long after, the memory of them pointed clearly to what I lacked in myself. I had a glimpse of this unity raised to a higher intellectual level – and with a 'spirituality' of saintliness – in hearing Mr Saklatvala at one meeting.

The note here, of course, is of one on the verge of conversion who rejects belief on the grounds of his own unsuitability and defects of character – the kind of excuse the religious never accept. But it is difficult to think that

9

O'Connor would have made a good communist: because beyond the decent comradeship of the members of the group in Wimbledon – or wherever – there lay the indecencies of the communist Church situated in Moscow – and he would have been bound to find this out.

Clearly he could never, on any terms, accept the idea of belonging to a community which was non-communist, least of all one which was bourgeois. He clings to his alienation for it is even advantageous in saving him from bourgeois attitudes.

A loner, he sees people from the outside; but he is also aware of them looking at him from the outside – which means that he has to put up a show for them to look at. It is as though he looked across a gulf at people standing on a stage and acting roles: but was also aware of them looking across that gulf at him standing on another stage opposite theirs, and acting his role – he sees them seeing him through their eyes. Moreover, he sees through the trickiness of his own act. He relates how he took advantage of the fact that at school he was called 'the Poet':

> The advantages of The Poet in sentimentally literary England, with its wealth of convention about the ineffectiveness of poets, their harmlessness and higher idiocy I naturally seized on. I readily subscribed to the idea that it was in the name of a higher calling that I became steadily more obtuse in the ordinary one.

The reader does not always feel sure that the person – whoever she or he may have been – for whom O'Connor was producing his effects, was taken in! Part of his self-consciousness is to be very self-critical. We are told that he cheats, plays truant, sponges, steals even. All this fits into the Chaplinesque role and is compulsively forgiven. To condemn him would be, too facilely, to show oneself a bourgeois.

There is much comedy in his insistence on the outsideness of people's physical features: as though nose, eyebrows, mouth, teeth were offensive-defensive weapons on the deck of some battleship:

> It was his face I first remember disliking. It was pudding, with implements of physical needs stuck on it, and in the ugly kind of coy functionalism early engineering displays. Its greatest tedium lay in the arched and permanently-raised eyebrows, giving him an expression of continuous and unfruitful astonishment; everything I said and did appeared to surprise him, till I became a wonder.

Clearly this book falls into the tradition of literature which is filled with compulsive hatred of the bourgeois. The bourgeois are contemptible because however well-meaning or kind or deserving they may be, they are materialistic utilitarians who identify happiness with the diminution of pain – the increase of comfort – in every aspect of their lives. What he understands supremely well is that to make the avoidance of pain the criterion of happiness anaesthetizes large areas of consciousness. What terrifies him is fear that the pursuit of painlessness may be a law of our natures.

There are really two kinds of happiness – the magical and the comfortable or pain-avoiding, the anaesthetic:

> *J'ai fait la magique étude*
> *Du bonheur, que nul n'élude.*

To me, these lines pose the contrast between happiness

which is a mysterious magical state of being and the compulsion to seek happiness (I may be misinterpreting Rimbaud, but never mind). The 'magical' happiness is a state of being which has nothing to do with comfort. O'Connor's life at Wimereux constituted magical happiness. Clearly happiness of this kind is only attainable in childhood. O'Connor cannot be said to have rediscovered his lost happiness. Yet he has consistently remained faithful to the memory of it, and has refused to accept any substitute for it. The title, *Memoirs of a Public Baby*, suggests that he throws himself on the mercy of a public to find for him the paradise of lost childhood, past time. What is poignant about his book is that he does not accept any compromise for the lost happiness which haunts these pages.

Stephen Spender
London, 1988

INTRODUCTION
TO FIRST EDITION
By STEPHEN SPENDER

No one would, I suppose, write an introduction to a book unless he honoured himself in doing so. Yet a book that did him honour should need no introduction. In appearing in front of Mr. Philip O'Connor's pages, I am specially conscious of this dilemma. His autobiography not only has qualities which take any passenger a very long ride; it also back-fires. It is saturated with the writer who has experiences, and views, and personality, of kinds despising literary gestures.

At the same time, perhaps just because this book is anti-literary, Mr. O'Connor and his publishers have honoured me with the request to introduce him to a public accustomed to 'literature'.

A word, to begin with, about the author. He is, as he describes himself, small, lithe, dark, concentrated, and totally absorbed in being Philip O'Connor. Meeting him, he is in sympathy with what is the truth, or the demonic, in you, completely intolerant of everything else.

In this book he relates that when young he wrote poems with extreme rapidity—almost without thinking —and then shot them off to editors, for whom, when they accepted these off-throwings, he felt a kind of dazed contempt. He is right in that his poems (some of which appear in anthologies) lacked most of the qualities which make achieved poems. They were just cuttings of Philip O'Connor's inner life. On the other hand, editors were right to recognise in them a concentration of original observations and vivid hallucinations, interesting and 'amusing', in their tragi-farcic way.

The poems were both good and not good. Good because they were automatic products of a most anti-mechanical personality, not good, because their author had no self-requirements of form or style by which he could 'work' at them. The most obvious thing about Philip O'Connor is that he has all the advantages and disadvantages of being original. He is utterly devoted to the kind of particularities which he takes to make up, for him, what is real. The criticism one might make is that, since he is incapable of being anything but himself for a single moment, and is, as far as conceivably possible, completely original, he cannot discover anything so objective as an artistic form. That explains the goodness and the badness of the poems, which disturbed him himself. For, surely, he would have been equally contemptuous of an editor who rejected them. They were, literally, bits of himself, and he knows himself as being alive. His writing is him, heated up—as he here reveals—with alcohol and stimulants.

The pattern, as such, is not unfamiliar. The twentieth century suffers from almost too much originality in art, and the 'systematic derangement of the senses' has become a cliché of living, as well as of poetry. The pursuit of 'real' living as against public and family shams, has become facile. Yet alcoholism and madness, just as much as bourgeois living, have aspects which—if one sees enough alcoholics and near-lunatics—can wear as hypocritical clothes as Lytton Strachey's mental image of the Prince Consort. A good many emperors who are proud to walk naked, wear very phoney skins.

The truth of the matter is that on every path of life, whether it leads to Presidencies of London Clubs or pubs or lunatic asylums, many are called but few are chosen. One characterises the group of those who are noisily 'called', but eventually one discovers that, in every group, it is only the chosen who count. The peculiarity of Philip O'Connor is that, on the crowded path he walks and portrays—of Fitzroy Street, drunks, tramps, Dionysians—he is absolutely the genuine article, one of the really chosen. He is without pose or affectation. He wears no mask. If he is correct in describing himself as schizoid, nevertheless he is single-minded in being his double-self. In life, as the extraordinary account of his marriage shows, he pursues the logic of the uninterruptedly unmasked and completely stated relationship to its nightmare end. In writing, his brain is a machine which registers each single impression anew.

At the very least, this book would add up to an interesting laboratory experiment in total sincerity. But luckily there is more than sincerity and originality confronting us here, more, that is, than Philip O'Connor. There is the touchstone of objective experiences in his childhood which have remained his connection with an outside reality of an impoverished, beaten-down, crazy kind, whereby he judges everyone, and himself. Possibly the most revealing passages in the book are those in which he describes the Tillieux family in Wimereux with whom, when he was at a very tender age, his mother 'parked' him for two years. Here (take it or leave it) is a key passage:

'Madame's affection for me was real, but it overstepped the bounds of decorum. I usually slept with her, and at night she would pinch my bottom giggling, which I didn't like, going nervously to the edge of the bed. But I liked the crash of her urine in the enamelled pail (which went up and down with us night and morning) before she got into bed. It was a great crash, but comforting, belonging to that order of noises which redress the balance from "spirituality". Her lack of "politeness" was to me a fundamental characteristic of her natural kindliness; good manners, particularly those cut, as it were, out of her own warm body by her immediate social superiors, were cruel in contrast, and truly vulgar.'

This gives the essentials of Philip O'Connor's pilgrimage. The physically coarse but true is held up as a criticism of inverted-commaed 'spirituality'; the vulgar, upheld against 'politeness'; and there is his self-identification with those who have been forced down by their 'superiors'. I would distrust the spirituality of any saint or bishop who did not see the force of this insistence. Saints who slept with lepers must have known about it. Even if one thinks that it could be comprehended without Madame Tillieux's forcible demonstrations, respectability is insidious. We should be grateful for anything that calls us loudly or sharply back to the vulgar un-vulgarity of the animal crashing around in and out of us.

Mr. O'Connor's tendency is to make an ideal of Madame Tillieux's behaviour, just as he makes an ideal of some abstract, coarse, physically and psychologically for-ever-exposed-to-the-truth, proletarian. Part of the interest of his autobiography is that it shows, like Ibsen's *The Wild Duck*, the catastrophic results of such idealism when applied to every moment of behaving. Yet if ruthlessly lived-out ideals are disproved by their results in personal relationships, they nevertheless can remain important as personal and social criticism. Ibsen flatters his presumably bourgeois audience when he shows that the fanatical idealist destroys a game of happy families. Criticism of hypocrisy does not lose its force because people are happy being hypocritical. The wild duck, like most of the naked emperors, was a phoney in his savage state, shut in a private loft.

Mr. O'Connor's force is that he is a critic of life around him, applying his ideals of truth and reality unceasingly. His criticism is not just based on the close observation of particulars, but he is, as it were, himself a particular, seeing everything from the point of view of his particularity. His autobiography shows that in real life he is something of a menace. He is aware of this; indeed, he is partly on the side of the reader against himself. He provides his own label for the reader, who is already equipped, with government, employer, wife and children all offering a dozen reasons for dismissing the man who even to himself goes labelled 'public baby'. Yet it is just as urgent to take him as to dismiss him, and for this reason I would like to conclude by inventing some more useful, if less amusing category for him than that of Public Baby.

What is his role in the lives of others, and in the life he describes? It is, I think, part angel, part demon. Whatever else Philip O'Connor does, he never 'sees life whole'. He sees it in little bits, and one of his aspects is certainly 'the spirit that denies'. That is to be demon. To put it mildly, he is the antithesis of Goethe. However, as the portrait of Madame Tillieux shows, he also has something to affirm. When he affirms he is angel.

17

What he denies is that one is anything but what one is at a particular moment. This is demonic, because it concentrates relationships into their moments, refuses to see them as parts within a whole myth that people have to create for themselves in order to take a part in the sham pageant of living. The demon tears them apart destructively into all their separate hells. He tells them that, to be honest, they should be mad.

At the other polarity, what Philip O'Connor affirms is that each moment of behaving and experiencing does exist, is as significant as all other moments, and has the same claim to be recognised; that the spirituality and politeness which pretend that some moments should be ignored is more vulgar than the coarsest facts and experiences which are real. This is angelic. The angel reminds us that we are what we are and that we should not construct views which betray our own being. Philosophies of life should not be made by skipping precisely that in us which has (in two senses) to be saved.

One cannot swallow Philip O'Connor or his book whole, because the whole is not his concern. On the other hand, a book that deepens our own reality is more valuable than many which give us generalised views and that comfort us with a smoothed-out false philosophy of the whole of life. This book reminds us of particular moments we have to deal with. It also shows us that personal truth is an infinite progression of saving and damning revelations. One does not have to agree with Philip O'Connor to see that his insights and his honesty are of the kind which gives us a grasp on ourselves. And often one has with him the sense that, more than most preachers, he offers body and spirit a blessed new chance. One can take this book and leave it and then take it again.

Part One

PREMATURITY

CHAPTER ONE

Had Mother had more of British 'weight' she could have availed herself of what advantages there were in being a Fallen Gentlewoman, or one in 'distressed circumstances'; but her infantile giggle, her utter lack of British social seriousness, were symptoms of a character and personality remote from that solemn status.

Her paternal grandfather came of a noble Irish family, and because of some indiscretion he had left the country and started life anew under another name in Burma; her father had married twice, the second time to a Dutch *bourgeoise* (whose family claimed a Statholder). They had prospered in Rangoon and later in Mysore and Bombay, one of them becoming Governor of Bengal; they were nearly all engaged in the Indian Civil Service. I have met only three: an aunt (Mother's stepsister) and her daughter and another cousin. The aunt, provoked especially by the squalor of our Kennington flat, was well endowed with the ornate nervously voluble refinement with which the British in India were correctly associated. It was she who, in a quarrel with Mother, ascribed her shortcomings (chiefest of which was her social fall) to the fact of her being a 'nigger', my aunt's strange name for a Burmese—in reference, I learned, to Mother's grandmother. This seems possible to me because of Mother's appearance. She was a very small woman, of about five feet in height (and wearing size three shoes), dark-skinned for a European, with large dark brown eyes the pupils of which were very soft and liquid like an oriental's, and dark-shadowed beneath, high cheek-bones and a snub nose; a pale line divided the red lip from the paler skin of her face. Her forehead was square and neat and upright, mannish, her hair blue-black and waved; her hands very small and beautifully articulated.

I think that Indians and Burmese are childlike in social intercourse and mature in emotional and sexual matters, and we the converse. Mother was remarkably childlike socially; she was devoid of civic consciousness, had no social drive with which to invade the field of thrown horsy gentlewomanhood. But emotionally, she had a gravity, a long rhythm, an access to deep feeling foreign to our sophisticated ways; and feeling in Mother so habitually reached the depths that she couldn't understand the hysteria caused by the same intensity of emotion on the rare occasions that western people feel it. She had no screech, but deep music. But this kind of emotion is unequipped with social expression in our system, and all that manifestly could be called adult in her was a deep, nostalgic depression whenever—and this was very rare—she caught a flash of her true social predicament. For her, 'adult' was synonymous with 'sad'.

Our visiting aunt's daughter, my cousin Polly, was a ravishingly beautiful and searingly snobbish girl whose every gesture was an act of segregation from the legion of her social inferiors—and their disgusting dwellings. This quasi-religious caste-consciousness was most pronounced and the least vulgarly so in my cousin Aidan; he was an unusually fine manifestation of the original crusading spirit possessed, however equivocally, by the core of

Empire-builders and administrators. A priest in the church of British Indian administration, he was a frail, delicately made man, of slight, exact gestures; quiet, continuous but precise movements; his thought of a flower-like delicacy in its reflective abeyance from obvious conclusions; his speech, as special as a scientist's disposal of rare specimens, petals of porcelain that had a thrillingly cleansing effect on my ear. So one may imagine that in the psycho-somatic process that allegedly extrovert man, the public administrator, becomes invert when the forms of his function outlast their significant content, with the emphasis, with men who feel morally called, on the extraordinary abstraction which their moral natures are forced to achieve. In the centre of his eyes were the signs—the vacancy—of a remarkable absence of 'central' consciousness: he had a great soul. His was a purer face than Mother's, more feminine where feminine in men means ascetic, saint-like and painfully remote from the world. His chronic abstractionism was well complemented to Indian concreteness.

She was born in Limerick in 1889. The family being fervently Roman Catholic, she was educated in a convent, and at nineteen she married. My father ('riff-raff' said Mother), according to Uncle Haslam to whom I'm indebted for most of the family history, was descended from the last High King of Ireland, and was royal in that he disliked a gainful occupation. He was a doctor of medicine, educated at Downside and Oxford, who never practised but preferred to be supported by Mother all the time he was with her. Mother told me that it had been bitter for her to suffer his marital behaviour after the wonder of his epistolatory wooing. I have never seen him,

23

perhaps fortunately, for he said he would drown in a
bucket any male child of his issue. But we knew him as
'the cad', and Mother told me various things about him:
that he had passions for clothes, for travelling, for jewel-
lery and for women—and for cleanliness; that he preferred China of all countries, that he wore bracelets, a
monocle, and continually changed his watches; that he
inspected the corners of hotel rooms on arriving and
raised hell about any dirt he found therein. He was a
total abstainer from alcohol and drank milk. He had once
spent a year in a monastery intending to take orders, but
had left to become, for a short time, stage-manager in a
theatre. He was frequently and openly unfaithful to
Mother, bringing his women home. Since Mother's
family were militarily heroic, my Uncle Sebastien having
been awarded the V.C., it was 'disgracefully' that he
refused to volunteer for military service in 1914 and was
conscripted for service as a naval surgeon in 1916. But
the Admiralty have confirmed neither this, nor the death
at sea in the same year that Mother attributed to him for
my benefit.

I imagine him to have been one of those men cursed
with an imaginative and esoteric morality of their own,
vulgarly called none at all by those outside the sainthood,
who find freedom in 'wickedness' because their expression of 'goodness' is impossibly complex and probably
illegal. He was no doubt lonely and sociable, sending his
compulsive self-consciousness to the winds in laughter
and love, and awaiting the return of the dark stranger in
solitude. This conception of him, and because in his
absence he was habitually maligned, produced an affection (in spite of the threat of drowning) which I later
transferred to the near-criminal class of bohemians with

whom I sojourned for a while. The state that I pictured was one where innocence, through inapplication, comes to be insulated by an increasingly vacant desert; meanwhile anti-social activities steadily nibble away at the once manifest integrity of childhood; finally the integrity collapses when the individual accepts the world's judgement frequently on an ethical plane far lower than his potential one—that of so-called reform; or he conducts crime respectably, which amounts to the same thing.

I have some doubt about my legitimacy because Mother, all the time I knew her, lived periodically with Uncle Haslam who behaved as a lover when she died; I resemble Uncle Haslam, and there must undoubtedly have been some reason such as this for Father's family refusing to see her. Further I was not allowed to see a photograph of him which, when I inadvertently did, was of Uncle Haslam in a straw-hat and early motor-car, but it may not have been the same photograph. Mother told me Uncle Sebastien had entrusted her to Uncle Haslam's care when he was called up.

When Mother married she went straight from convent and hyper-conventional Anglo-Indian home to the charming and amoral Irish doctor who, being 'the world' to her, was also a warning against further penetration in it. In her morning gossips with us in bed she always spoke, as in the poetry of a past life, of her Indian childhood; those days were the happiest and morally best. Away from home she played at being grown up as in an artful masquerade, the emotion and the manner being copied. And in the home circle, our domestic encampment where we played Red Indians against the world, she would giggle at the skill of her performances; in the same way in my teens I would act the grown-up gentleman making in the mirror a medley of adult faces, judicial, scrutinising, insinuating, cynical, ironical, portentous-noble, Prussian dead-pan, degenerate-sophisticated faces, screaming with laughter to break them and, by magical proxy, their British or filmic models.

Of her married life Mother spoke rarely, and always in the voice of as much maturity (and sadness) as she ever attained to. Flatly—for it had been more of a decision than a conviction—as though brushing away a repellent insect, she would say, 'A cad'. But she had loved, and perhaps adored him. My father had been, she'd say, a wonderfully skilled surgeon, his taste in clothes impeccable, his love-letters intoxicating: handsome, tall, slim, without ugly hairs on his chest, with beautiful manners, a fine dancer, altogether a man of grace, wit and elegance. My sister said that Mother had only twice 'suffered' sexual intercourse: once for her and once for me. Mother believed in virginity alleviated by scandal. She liked to be shocked.

This anti-sexuality and pruriency intensified the temperature and the colour, and also the (*anglice*) eccentricity of her way of life: her childishness, the squalor in which she lived, her adoration of the Virgin Mary with whom she babbled on the most intimate terms, her passion for black coffee, for original sweetmeats (her favourite was made of Nestlé's milk, coconut and cocoa, mashed) her primitively exotic cooking; all were characteristics which served what apparently was a purpose of withdrawal from the society of her social equals. But hers was no self-conscious social catastrophe; though a snob in the simplest girl-guide sense of the word she was happiest and most at ease—true, with a little patronage, but not much—with the poorest working-class people and she lived with them in their dirtiest slums for the only happy years of her life I witnessed. In none was 'infantile regression' more evident: hence my desire to soften the rigid norm by whose standard the case is reduced to technical 'neurosis'. Those who withdraw from normality may have better reasons for so doing than are apparent to the 'normal world's' secular priests.

She had a sincere loathing of the English middle-class —my best inheritance from her—which she as sincerely feared for its terrifying vulgarity, its perfected lack of sensibility and its bewildering equivocation. She loathed particularly the women, who profoundly embarrassed her. But the men made her titter; she was aware of artificial 'weight'.

For twenty years or more until her death poverty was her exciting adventure, and mushrooms, chocolate liqueurs, Turkish cigarettes, artichokes, chickens, love—of her children, the Virgin Mary, her Mother and Baby Jesus— the lovely rewards of the struggle. To go marketing with Mother (I remember the Waterloo Road) was to apprehend with all the senses the beauty of food; only when one grew up did it gain its utilitarian attributes at the expense of all else. She haggled delightedly over everything, and departed as though from an embrace with the fascinated vendor. She believed in gentlemen at street corners selling gold watches for sixpence. She was so great that she believed in every kind of rogue provided he didn't look prosperous; and together we played at everything, even at not eating and at flitting round by moonlight. Her happiness seemed to increase in proportion to the wretchedness of her circumstances.

My sister was born in a train entering Paris seven years before me, and was called Désirée in definition of her parental reception. She was a very pretty, volatile girl, perhaps prematurely objective in emotional matters. She'd loved Father very much, and had travelled with him and Mother continuously before my birth. The end of Mother's resources, his reputed conscription, and his affection for her all appear to have coincided, in the year of my birth.

I was delivered with great difficulty, a little prematurely and in the expectation of being twins, in Leighton Buzzard, by the King's physician, said Mother, and while an air-raid was over London; in an aura, furthermore, of a gipsy's prophecy of fame. She provided me with four names reminiscent of a Gilbert and Sullivan overture. As soon as she recovered we moved to Pinner, and thence to Yeovil. She must still have had a little capital, for there she founded the 'Somerset Cigarette Agency' and secured a government contract for the cigarettes that she admitted to be very bad: she had no morals of the kind to enforce the making of good cigarettes. They were made in a red-carpeted room in London, near the Savoy Hotel, where she employed about twenty girls. I remember making one in a tube sitting on her lap. But the company failed and was replaced by 'Phildes' *Sebasdes* Products Ltd.', portmanteauing my name and my sister's. This also foundered quickly, and Mother then fought one of the 'Big Five' banks, lost her case, and with it Uncle Haslam's credulously invested few thousands of pounds. She was declared bankrupt. The boxful of the papers of the case followed us down the years and with it the bank was remembered as the first of Mother's long list of 'crooks'. All these crooks began their terms of office as people who were 'straight as a die', a 'sahib', 'clean' people, and so on but usually fell after a few months. It was down the large flight of stone steps from our house in Yeovil that I ran to offer my madly-beloved toy piano to passers-by, and later my train: and the desire to give it away was incident with the love of it. Such an emotion has not recurred.

When the war ended we came to London, staying at first in a vast hotel and then somewhere in the Cromwell Road: the pillared porticoes of the hotel were always magnificent for me; so was the vast apartment within wherein one ran full speed from huge settee to embedding arm-chair, across thick carpets, with low luscious lights from a standard-lamp. The high ceiling, the great room, made for me the early feeling, the peculiarly light freedom of 'proper living', and I have a consciousness immediately evoked by anything similar—a consciousness that has only briefly lived, and is completely different to that of the existentialism of poverty. A concomitant of it is an extra verbal fluency—legato as opposed to the staccato dashes and dots caused by inhibiting poverty; also a relaxation as found in wine, and a fine privacy and aloofness. Early memories are all housed in this predominant quality, an enfolding ecclesiastical hush, from which, in my mendicant days ambling through Mayfair in warm summer evenings, I would hear the soft mice within squeak euphoniously, dissolving butter on my ear. In poverty, in confinement, the echoes from childhood tear my speech with contradiction, and equivocation becomes spontaneous; moreover my 'selfishness' comes from an unbreakable emotional attachment to this original luxury, of which Mother carried the spiritualised odour always.

There is an early photograph of me, or there was, before which I would later watch artfully the artless affection with which I would gaze upon my image, as upon a lost beloved child, whose eyes were huge with nervous receptivity of an already suspected world, whose lips had that ominous looseness well expressed in the years after; a 'beautiful' child, too nervous, and possessed of a cryptic weakness, as though strength had been deflected from its natural channels. One could have said of this child that he had an ignorance of certain things which he should not lose.

CHAPTER TWO

It was probably in 1919 that we crossed to France:
Mother, my sister, my nurse, Dora, and myself.
We crossed at night, on a rough sea; the two funnels
of the boat, dutifully belching clouds of illuminated smoke
with the deck spread out like a tray around them. The
ship shuddered, and I couldn't see why the soft water
didn't let the ship go through it. Mother was sick.

We went to Paris. We crossed a big *place*, with greater
brio than London, and with the items of traffic contributing to it being more distinguished, in a greater separation
from each other; the result was more brilliant, and I
conceived an immediate affection for the long green
snub-nosed buses so dashingly plying across the surface
of the *place*. Moreover, the sky was more apparent in
Paris, and everything freshened by it. But we stood a long
while on the brink of the *place* before, tightly clutched,
we ran. We went to Madame Antoine's, a friend of
Mother's, who lived in a many-small-roomed flat near
the *place*. In a small *salon* were divans by the walls
covered with bright silk cushions. The wallpaper and the
carpet were brilliant and the air scented. Madame was
small, plump and silk-clad, and possessed of an architectural breast or bosom, to which she clasped me in what I
first sensed as being a purely 'technical 'embrace. It
disconcerted me, to find me so much a mere object, and
in some logical association with the alien bosom, I split

31

open one of her bright silk cushions to discover what was inside. Madame was shrill-voiced in indignation but, what was worse, Mother, I felt with a loss of principle (for Mother cared little about cushions) pretended to share her indignation; this was perhaps the first time I noticed a conspiracy necessitating duplicity in the strange grown-up world.

In Paris we stayed at the Hotel du Louvre, which appeared to me to be a very luxurious place. The level of the floor where our bed stood was higher than the rest of the room; the sheets were silk or at least extremely soft, for I awoke next morning in these sheets with my head on my mother's bare breast, as the maid arrived with breakfast; this was the last time I saw Mother's breast.

We very soon went to Wimereux, I don't know why. Wimereux is a little seaside place about five kilometres from Boulogne-sur-mer, where many retired English people stayed at that time. We rented an apartment near the level crossing, on the ground floor with a walled garden behind; the garden was sunny. Mother had a sewing machine. It was a nice house, of dark red brick, with a muslin-curtained window looking on to the street. But we soon moved to Madame Tillieux' teashop, in the rue Carnot, the main road of the little town.

It was in the early part of our stay at Madame Tillieux' that I first became aware of our family's distinction from the rest of the world, and in that way weaker; an observation heightened by Mother's new 'economic manner', one of suave astuteness, God-approved and Virgin-Mary-advised. The beginnings of her sentences in this manner were invariably 'ah' sounding, especially in her bad French; she was busy in waving away expected objections. Then her words were heavy with a certainty that appeared almost to pain her with its acuteness. The other person would appear to me to be big and wrongly immovable. I felt frightened for Mother in her difficulty. The other people demanded; creditors were still vague to me, and atmosphere; but the atmosphere was thick enough to make 'home' too strangely a refuge, and a refuge closer to our persons than a house, a place; for we had already had so many. 'Home' was Mother, and then her trunk, her coffee-pot, etc. When I saw my first crib in the church at the end of the town, strawed, prettily lit, intimate and yellow-glowing, I saw what I felt was like our home, still and bright within. So any of our homes, and now this one at Madame Tillieux', was ruddy-lit, still, warm, thick with us and stoved by Mother.

One day the 'shock-definition' of our home came to me. A light wind and a bright sun, on a fine morning, were round us on the downs above the sea between Boulogne and Wimereux. We had gone to pick mushrooms, walking from Wimereux along the long winding road built, it seemed, on a roof above the sea, arching its back as it wound high along; the telegraph wires hummed with sounds seeming to come from a long way away and to be on their way to somewhere a long way away, and narrow fields of clover were between them and the cliff edge. I put my nose in the clover and had a great meal of it down my nose. Once Mother had gone too far ahead with my sister, and my strange compulsion not to be seen wanting her made me not run quickly after her as I naturally would have done, but to affect not to notice, and when she called I came uncaring. We had picked a big bag of mushrooms. But after the sun and wind and the sea's sounds, we seemed to dive into our little apartment and fry the mushrooms quickly and eat them as though we'd stolen them from the enemy's world. We ate them in a way different from all other meals, and the room was smaller, stiller, hotter, brighter than all rooms before it had been. We must have sensed a stillness between the sounds of the cutlery on the plates, a descriptive stillness or one introducing some approaching dirge of experience—the peace of life was breaking, as though soon we would see the sea.

Out of the glow emanating from Mother sometimes an object would stand alone. My eye would travel along the grain, a cold road of hard, shining brown wood, would loiter at particles of dust; the road would end at a violent vertical, which would be a chair, then again the velvet seat would bristle with millions of red hairs; and it was in such a material that I could lose myself, as though deserted, in a meaningless, depressingly alien world. Strangers would frighten me similarly, but more: a red face, so much more of material than of personal flesh, would open and close, would emit violent sounds and clang in uneven rhythms; I would be pressed to it with great sweeps of arms and legs, and boisterous shouts.

I was suddenly aware of my sister; she had until now been near enough, as a subsidiary and adoring mother, to have failed to achieve that triumph, personality, which we accord to even beloved equals in the social strife. But now she distinguished herself into my consciousness by the cruel process of personalisation, bewildering, alarming and exciting. She shot up, in my peaceful observation, into a metallic flower with angled, cryptic arms, with a painful brightness brightest when it laughed in the conventions of affection but with the content of

34

that enmity that different sex is assumed to necessitate. I think she was then entering Mother's confidence, and that much of the bared-teethed laughing and athletic fun which she was now showing was prompted by her elation in her premature understanding of money, the difficult tactics of survival, and perhaps the confidence of Mother's sorrows and Father's wickedness. She acquired a martial vivacity that became more pronounced as it came, ultimately successfully, to separate her feelings from her expressions. A lever of what amounted to our estrangement was a sudden development of childish sexuality between us. She would lie on her back and hold me above her and then suddenly let me drop between her legs; I liked the feeling, but couldn't properly distinguish between affection and sexuality, and was frightened at a strange element of coldness in her in these games. I felt stupid, therefore, and she felt brilliant. I began to fear her, and she began to tease me.

It was in Wimereux about this time (I was about three) that a later nightmare may have originated, in which I was nursed by a gorilla in a circus. The nightmare consisted of my trying to leave the gorilla but being unable to because of his soft brown eyes, which lovingly begged me not to go; but the matter is very mixed, for later my guardian also reminded me of the gorilla. Another part of the dream which antedates him, was imagining myself in a caravan with two people making love at the other end. Learning of this, Mother, for years afterwards, read me Ballantyne's *Gorilla Hunters* to quieten my fears. Recently I saw something resembling my dream figure in Jean Marais' 'Beast'. But I have a lasting fear of monkeys as well, feeling horribly near to them and that I have a secret they might discover which would involve me in some unconscious activity consequent upon the discovery of a bond between us.

In my third year my nurse dropped me twenty feet from a window on to a stone courtyard. She also pulled me by the hair out of a hot bath and since Mother could no longer afford her, she was sent back to England. I think she was little more than fourteen or fifteen, and probably was rarely paid.

When we had been at Madame Tillieux' perhaps two months Mother told me she must leave me but would return very soon. But she stayed away for two years. Hence, she implanted in my mind a very detailed abstraction of herself to which, when she returned, she failed to approximate; she gradually became predominantly what others were not. She left in me the embryo of an ideal of delicacy impossible to find in anyone ever after except in L., for my unsatisfied yearning for her recoiled upon myself, and behind a protective skin made impossible demands from others. I remembered the feel of her hands like living leaves on me so that when others touched me, the association aroused immediately an excruciating hope and a baleful disappointment that developed into a neurasthenic *noli me tangere*. My skin developed a frantic intelligence of contact that short-circuited satisfaction from any contact, the hope being frightened out of existence by the sharp memory that this was not the one, the real thing; the nearest approaches are water, a warm bath, and wind on my wet body.

Her movements became indefinitely wonderful, only approached in finely articulated music; they had a logic and an ease, a rhythm and flow that constituted happiness for those present. By comparison, Madame Tillieux' touch was rough, and her skin hard and shiny so that it

36

slithered superficially where Mother's would penetrate pore by pore; for emphasis, Madame would clutch which made me sick and strange. Her movements were the comic horizontal falling here and there of a badly packed parcel, but a parcel of strange things never to be discovered by one outside her own family. Mother's eyes became, in memory, houses in which I gradually seemed to dwell; they were of an animal melancholy like those of my gorilla, having the quality of appearing to recede from me as they watched—an appearance of the infinite recession of the pupils, while tears flooded them.

Mother's departure meant my sudden dropping from the more delicate grace and status of (I think) paying guest to abandoned child and dependent; for Mother sent no money for my upbringing in the two years she was away. She had none. I landed, it seemed, one morning, alone on the bright-tiled floor of the *salle à manger*, a small nervous vertical piece of person on a huge hard expanse from which sprang several big and frightening other verticals.

Madam Tillieux came of a peasant family. She supported herself and four children by means of the teashop, which was also a *pâtisserie* and *confiserie*, catering largely for English visitors. On her ruddy kindly face were the fine lines of economically induced expressions, but they had not eaten away their warm, kindly background. Her intelligent blue eyes were warm and kind, almost hot blue, and the arithmetic calculations shown in the lines of her face were dissolved as in the sunrise of her affectionate and comfortable, and comforting smile. She looked very early with love at me. Compared with Mother she appeared to wear 'outside' as flesh that thing which Mother had 'inside' as soul. Mother's ways were

distinctly ladylike; and yet the difference was not so
very great, except in that intelligence and degree
of tenderness natural to a mother. But her public
manner was very different—Madame, floridly emotional,
Mother, suave (somewhat affectedly so, in her business-
woman role) but in a softer key, and her voice soothed
whereas Madame's excited. Mother was private, and had
an excelling convention of social reflex; Madame was
public, and her movements married with those of the
crowd. So it was, I remembered later, Mother who
cheated Madame. Madame in a way was more deplorably
vulnerable, because her flesh was more feeling, because
her feeling was more part of her flesh, than Mother, who
had a breeding which regulated her reactions. So when
Madame had a crochet needle embedded in her thumb I
felt faint and sick with horror, as though part of her true
self had been wounded; whereas a similar accident happening to Mother would have produced a clear emotional
response. Madame's maternalism then was outside,
shining from her red scrubbed skin; I think it induced in
me an unorthodox and rather tragic impulsion to have
my soul in my actions, my brain 'in my body', and
hampered me in the acquisition of my proper class characteristic—of body as vehicle, of soul as elixir of what
lower-class people have as body; it gave me ambitions to
proletarianism, because the stimulating effect of Madame
was terrific, as was the live atmosphere in general of the
near working-class France I was to live in for three or
four years. I failed to make the proper departmentalis-
ation of the self; soul, heart, body, brain: I failed, in fact,
to hold an illusion which collectively held is a social
tragedy, but individually, provides a technique for social
competition. It is true that she elevated herself a little

above her human contacts, making a small investment in 'decency' for economic purposes, but on the other hand she expected and received a good deal of a love and affection from humanity that, in economic terms, was a dead loss. From her I gained my first and everlasting taste of the economy of working-class behaviour, of, ultimately, its *finesse* superior, in a profound way, to the highest social concoctions of sensitivity that the high-bred have developed. Their delicacy in emotional matters, I soon became aware, was infinite, was right. At its best this is a heavy and fairly self-conscious technique of good taste in the upper classes. From three to six I 'knew where I was', in spite of, because of, Mother's absence; the social orientation acquired a basic emphasis against the personal one: but the matter was not happily worked out; indeed, it created the problem. My life with her was more regulated than it was ever to be after; though, as she said, I was '*jamais content*'.

If Madame was easily, peacefully in the way of social elevation, three of her four children were in the current to increase that elevation; but differently. Jean, at the university, chose intellectual advancement; Jeanette, afflicted with brilliance quite indefinable except literally that she sparkled, was rehearsing the social way, in terms of marketable personality; Pierrot, the youngest, sulked against this elevation; but paradoxically, he did so in such a way that, his heart cut off from its sentimental yearnings, he manifested it more successfully than the rest. Berthe, the younger sister, chose the way of God, of progressive detachment from life. My next indoctrination was a fear and a dislike of those who tried to rise socially, because I disliked Jeannette and precisely for those characteristics ('brilliance') which were the agents

39

of it. The enamels of propriety were already hardening on her; she 'dealt with' people, seeing them through assessing eyes. She would enter the business world of the heart, and marry on that basis; and already (at around fourteen) she had a suggestion of that jeering, if skilfully muted, belligerency of the economic animal, whose solitude is a material triumph and a melodramatic tragedy. She would make a fine fat soul for herself, and in increasingly better circumstances have increasingly fashionable *angsts*. Her nose was long and sharp, like her chin, her eyes brightly cold, her movements were 'antarctic', like a glass puppet's, with a ring and a nipped bounce in them; she played the piano with the exquisitely agonising accuracy of a dentist extracting teeth.

I grew very fond of Pierrot who was three years my senior, but I loved Berthe even more. Though pudding-faced and small-pocked she was to me infinitely more beautiful than Jeannette; in such contexts children have the eyes of artists, so that Jeannette was a Van Dongen, while Berthe was a Flemish Madonna. There was also Grand'mère who sat by the stove and restricted her speech to the announcements of her physical needs. But in her eyes one could find whatever one sought; that I was happy seems contradicted by the amount I did look for in them, as into wishing-wells for the solution of a problem.

There were three *salles* separated by folding doors on the ground floor of Madame Tillieux' house—she bought it many years later. The front, on the street, was the shop and first tea-room. On the left, facing the street, were the cakes—*Gâteaux-bâteaux*, Calais cakes, éclairs; on the right, jars of sweets, sugared almonds, Chocolate *Rochet*, *Pierrot-Gourmand*, *sucre-d'orge;* the smell was heavy heaven. At the little tables in the shop itself the most chic connoisseurs of *pâtisseries* discussed quickly the delicious *gâteaux*, eating with such shamelessness—I mean, to me, then, when I was not eating—as to make me hate them; with hatred and envy I watched their big white teeth dipping sheerly into the creams and biscuitry, their lips proudly curve and pensively fold over the sweet crumbles, their cream-coated tongues dart like acquisitive rabbits from red hutches. The second *salle* was darker, haunted by a large aspidistra and certain dark objects in the corner which I never was able to see. Here the English, mousily talking, ate more sacredly; I walked always straight through this strange *salle*, parquet-floored unlike the others. The third was our living-room, French-stoved at the end of a very long chimney, to the left of which big-moustached M. Tillieux, a stern, military-looking man, hung in effigy. We faced him at evening prayers, going straight through his face to God: '*Marie, Mère de Dieu, priez pour nous, pêcheurs*, etc.' We were sinners every evening. To the left was a long window running the whole length of the wall, with a built-in settle; the yard lay outside.

The three *salles* provided three stages of undress from shop etiquette; I watched Maman rising redfaced from a meal, acquiring her ostensibly uneager waddle in the middle *salle*, her bright shopkeeping face—'social service'—in the shop; I would hear her tones of urbane reflectiveness upon her cakes. On the return, the walk was quicker, the smile doffed, a private look substituted; sometimes she would scratch under her skirt at the entrance to the living-room—perhaps to rehumanise herself; at this, Jeannette would exclaim 'Maman!' pleased with her ability to sound so shocked; and Maman was pleased so to be able to please Jeannette; as when she chewed chicken bones, she would excuse herself with the phrase '*en famille*'.

Her public and her private modes were clearly planted in my mind; I couldn't understand why one should be so energetically affectionate to strangers; Maman was infinitely patient while they slowly masticated one cake after another in their minds' mouths, preening themselves the while on some spiritual superiority they associated with such exact gourmandise. If the English eat sentimentally, even anthropomorphically, the French, it seems to me, eat cruelly, showing their teeth more, tasting dreadfully in contrast to our faithful and superstitious swallowing. But that kind of cruelty is art. Maman's meals were sacred, but in this case the cooking justified the solemnity. Grace first, then the big round loaf: Maman, eyes upward, would make the sign of the cross with her knife on its bottom, then cut; then the big soup-tureen; Sundays, a *gâteau* at the end; my elbows would be banged twice on the table if I put them there. I would stare hard at people while eating, for the whole personality is manifested, even magnified, there, with its declaration of rights and needs, eyes secretly wandering from one face to another, a wealth of facial expression with the emphatic surfaces becoming comically or frighteningly mechanical. Berthe looked sad at mealtimes; Jeannette often brilliant, like a 'cut'-glass mug. It was at table that I first smelled slightly the atmosphere of my developing dependence on Maman; and it was there that I first established my personal right, until, gradually edging my way into acceptance, my dinner-table status became general.

The little bee-like trams shuddering in rigidity and making a noise like an avalanche of iron, with bells clang-

ing and screaming on their rails, rushed through the rue
Carnot to their terminus at the end of the town, where
they stood seraphically quiet before the next charge.
Some of the happiest times of my life were spent in these
trams on the weekly cake-buying expedition to Boulogne.
The whole family would see us off at the door, Maman
carrying a high pile of empty cake-cartons. The combined groan and humming vibration seethed through me
as we set off, the little beast of a vehicle so intelligently
and eccentrically tilting round at the bends, bobbing up
and down on the straights. On great occasions there'd be
a hold-up midway for the 'Grand' Marée', when a white
high wall of spumy sea would come crashing at the
windows in myriads of drops, pouring down the glass as
though from a cloudburst, the sea booming and singing
fresh from below, where the storm raged. The tram
would calculate when it could dart forward in between
the big waves. In calm weather our tram would wait for
the tram coming the other way; a queer silence, the sea
singing, biscuity talk in the sun-drenched interior, air
fresh as whisky, and then a silence—the distant moan,
song, rumble, clatter of the other tram; the impressively
dashing salutations of the drivers, manœuvring of the
conductor-arms, and off again. Where the trams met at
the loop in the rail was always the most exposed place in
the world; the sea twinkled on our right miles and miles
in the distance, the gulls shrieked us out of our cosy
compartment; behind, the wide light green of the dune-
fields, and trams protectively housing their so compact
occupants, so small in the wide, high place. In Boulogne
the driver was bad-tempered, banging his bell continuously through the press of people, a barrage of them
raucous with the shrill cries of the fisherwomen with big

baskets crying '*Maquereaux, maquereaux frais*'. We would alight before a smart little *confiserie;* and once, as Maman stepped off I caught a stranger's glimpse of her, and inwardly almost wept at her tightly-gathered homeliness and seeming helplessness among so many strangers, and at her shabbiness. On some nice principle, I think, Maman was always badly dressed—perhaps in faithfulness to her dead husband, but she seemed so particularly when we met the silky-clothed lady of this *confiserie;* her longish face would be lengthened for the smile at the little boy and she'd exasperate me by pretending to expect a reasoned reply to some unfathomably senseless question; and this, to my honour, I never forgave her despite the *gâteau* she'd give me in her attempt to cover her tracks.

When I saw the trams again at fourteen, those splinters of my educated concept of them bore no resemblance to the wonders of my infancy; as D. H. Lawrence only too truly said (in as many words), we're successfully taught to know reality away.

Madame's affection for me was real, but it overstepped the bounds of decorum. I usually slept with her, and at night she would pinch my bottom giggling, which I didn't like, going nervously to the edge of the bed. But I liked the crash of her urine in the enamelled pail (which went up and down with us night and morning) before she got into bed. It was a great crash, but comforting, belonging to that order of noises which redress the balance from 'spirituality'. Her lack of '*politesse*' was to me a fundamental characteristic of her natural kindliness; good manners, particularly those cut, as it were, out of her own warm body by her immediate social superiors, were cruel in contrast, and truly vulgar.

Every quarter day Maman wept before the landlord; I was employed as the last ounce to her burden of responsibility, the one enabling her regularly to cry: *'J'ai cinq enfants, Monsieur,'* my shoulder supporting her bereaved widow's hand.

The shop was part of the street and furthest from my affections; nearest was the chicken-run in the backyard. I tried to sleep there when I collected eggs, liking the smell of the droppings. I loved the hens; their sharp, matronly scrutiny out of eyes planted like the slits in castles, their eccentric movements expressing an uncompromising thoroughness of purpose and simplicity that would become funny if I were to lose those qualities myself. My first sense of a perfect shape was aroused by a boiled egg in artificial light, its mound slowly undressed of the wavy-edged petticoat of steam, and where the rope-shaped edge of steam left the mat wall of the egg was perfection; and then again where it towered to its final, self-enclosing apex. Next came a night-light, whose flame was hope, courage, warmth and clarity afloat on a saucer of water; a tiny petal-flame, one of Lawrence's flames, taken to heart.

Another love—I had plenty—was Folette, the ageing bitch who lay all day motionless in the yard, simmering in the sun; a dirty white, big, fat dog with a wet red nose and red-rimmed eyes; eyes like old people's, innocent of the heart, eyes, rather, that pulled the heart to her and made one put one's arms round her in adoration of something that so much lacked belligerency. Folette and the hens were opposite to adults possessed of the organising drive; I knew my world at first sight, that of Folette and the hens, into which Berthe would be allowed, qualified by her social sickness, and Pierrot because of his social sulk.

45

The beach at Wimereux is very white and very wide. The sea spreads from one's feet to the sky: the horizon is like one's eyes brimmed with tears, an ecstasy of horizontality. Behind the beach the dunes rise with the fine breeding of true wind-sculpture, nobly and mournfully with sparse grasses shivering atop; the dunes to the song of the sea is a conversation one can hear but not interrupt; a thin river like a silver wireworm pattered into the sea from Wimereux; its warm clear water stupidly washed immaculate pebbles; the surface was so exactly like laughter as to make one feel laughter at the sight of it. A little higher on the dunes was a rusty railway trolley; standing on the trolley and facing the sea and sky I conducted it to far places, resolutely, transforming the distance and the stillness into infinite speed; at twilight Pierrot and I left the earth; we entered a dreamy state, where the mind sinks into the body like water back into sands, refreshing to both, the physical thinking state where the body talks, as in dancing. I didn't successfully return from the journeys on the trolley; something of the meaning of that play-metaphor informed my being; real journeys were a scratch on the skin of that one, and involved only a fraction of me. The expression of the trolley has something in common with that of church gargoyles—a journey at the expense of fear. A drainpipe lay beside our trolley, and, perhaps in rehearsal for the greatest show on earth, Reality, we would crawl through it. Pierrot was better at this than I.

If we returned from the trolley in time, we would fish for eels through the cracks in the boards of the little bridge by the *mairie*, Pierrot doing the fishing and I the admiring. Memories of twilight in Wimereux return home in a glass of wine; little beans of warmth from the heart's

pod pop throughout the network of nerves to the mne-
monic nerve-stations; I inhale accompanied by the sound
of the sea in recession, exhale with the sea coming in; a
fantasy of the mauve of evening with the dimmest stains
of rusty red on the horizon, dissolve the walls of consciousness in the teeth of 'the body' and 'the world'. I
recollect that the Virgin Mary's cloak in the church
nearby was made of evening mauve; perhaps it's the
Roman Catholic emotion.

To be truthful—looking back—the sun slivered, on
the blue waves, flashing dazzlingly, was better and
happier. It called out love and laughter, and these are
more delicate, more refined than sorrow, an emotion too
highly esteemed because of our impression of its pomp.
Like the sun on the waves was the fun-flash in Pierrot's
eyes, as he played, his heart engaged, the church and the
good hounded out by the pagan. And before my spontaneity became deliberate, Pierrot and I found a physical
consummation for our joint affection; the vestments of
sophistication were lacking.

I began to notice different degrees of intimacy between
people. I can barely remember how Maman was dressed
but can feel the texture of her clothes; whereas M. Leroy,
her cousin, the tobacconist at the end of the rue Carnot,
shone in double-breasted serge, a stiff white collar and
large tie. Maman's face, the one I remember, is a face of
expressions more than features; M. Leroy's is lustrous
lobster-coloured surmounted with thick black pointed
moustaches, and with big eyebrows; his eyes are dark
and hot (the '*tabac*' is also a *bistro*); his face is usually
worn stiff, and it can crack into very few expressions—
the thick lines in it showing the routine ones. He is big,
broad, tall, erect, and makes 'a manner'. His wife is

complementarily 'splendid' and vacuous, an elegant figure in a hackneyed mode, big, not fat, her hair most 'done', florid and flashing, while elegance, the censor of mirth, channels her smiling into small, neo-ladylike constrictions. They move comically as a pair, the emphasis mostly from the hips, which waggle. Their expressions are very public; Monsieur, dully handsome, a weight on the soul. But his *tabac-bistro* is not so with its stink of French tobacco, wines and beer, pungent periodicals and papers, its thick voices, red faces and yearning declamation. Maman remains a haze of familiar attributes, Monsieur Leroy an exact portrait of an unknown.

Moreover, I was grievously aware of 'distinction' in the Leroys, denoted in pauses of great value between phrases (*'il achève sa phrase'*), in dramatic swings from the hips, in abruptly fateful hurlings out of the hand to the departmental skies; Madam L's glassy coo threaded somewhat angularly through his sausage-sentences. They arranged their behaviour, and had no natural contact. Life was arrested in their presence, and a psychic hiccough born which, organised and better scored, flowers into the English cough. I have seen the Leroys in groups by Le Douanier Rousseau.

Maman was the stove; Berthe my soul's bath, literally so, for she bathed my body every Saturday night, wiping me tenderly on her lap and looking with eyes softly blue at me, with love. Berthe was sad for something not there, her father perhaps, for she would have been a father's favourite daughter and Jeannette would have come to the fore at his death, as one of the kind who, missing the father association, can brilliantly 'deal' with men. I was sad in the same way, and we resembled opposite banks of a river with our hearts and the absent ones joined in the water flowing between us, and we were sometimes obstructed by hideous craft on the water. Moreover we could never meet; we ached for something, and tones were more expressive than words. She bathed my body, treating it reverently not as me but as my representative; me, she recommended to God and for her sake I may even have believed in him for a while—I could well associate the semi-consciousness of love with divinity. Her touch—my speciality—could be heavier than several feathers intelligently articulated as fingers, but resting longer and warmer (Jeannette's was clever with the same brisk intelligence with which she rapped out her stalactitic melodies on the piano). But Berthe wanted to take something from me and put it in a special place, a grand safe where hers too rested; her eyes sidled gently by this world, guarded by the kind of haze you might see in a peasant girl's religious rapture.

She kissed me to bed like a consecration, her lips gentle, coolish, soft, her voice a holy loving whisper as from far within her, and she arranged my arms crosswise on my chest. No harm can come to one if one's loved, because that makes one intelligent, and from Berthe I learnt bliss—a great sea of bliss in the safety of women and its complement, hatred of the equivocally named 'male principle' which implies the confounding of love with money.

An icon in my memory depicts myself on a towel on Berthe's lap in the evening light to the right of the cherry-red French stove, the tin bath at her feet, her little bits of lip-work dropping gently on my ears; and with it there is another in which I am walking with Jeannette who carries a bucket with ice in it, tapping hard with her

49

high heels on the pavement in bitter January in a biting wind, the tip of her nose characteristically red, and her eyes sharp.

Berthe's pious soul was the lovely, if heavy cloud condensing frequently into big, slow-falling tears down a cheek whose plainness was so vividly beauty to me. The cloud floated above all irritations of family life and made her to others sometimes infuriatingly immune to their tight problems. It was to make contact that Maman broke out into wild anger sometimes, once nearly throwing an iron at her; Berthe was then as helpless as a medium.

M. Jules was a French sportsman who occasionally stayed with us, a Tartarin, a cautious pocket-huntsman of pigeons and seagulls, chubby and melancholic. One day he staged a scene with me in which I was to play the role of wondering child to his big-game huntsman; as soon as I realised what he wanted, I painfully contrived some tears of admiration (assisted by the wind); he realised that this sacrifice bored me and compensated me with a big wooden omnibus. I seized it epileptically in the middle-*salle*, and after a few moments knew, in a flood of shame, scarlet-cheeked, that I'd completely forgotten Maman, standing a little way away observing me (probably not with this thought); and running to her, I buried my face in her black overall. It was my first seduction by things from people, the first experience of the fiercer, keen heart-beat of erotic-acquisitive lust.

Memories darken in their recession; there's a picture, for instance, of a wicker basket by rushes near a river— yet I think I read Genesis much later. I'd strain my eyes under closed lids, pressing the eyeballs hard for the stars to resolve into a clear picture, always impossible: in

memory, I think very early ones, I sense the ocular
experience slowly dissolving into the auricular one—
the image becomes a vague shadow, almost audibly
mumbling in the texture of its shape. From Wimereux
then come primary colours, reds and blues mostly: a
brown-sailed fishing-boat, a toy one, whose shape was so
containing, the bows so perfectly and kindly resistant to
the water. I experienced ecstasies over a hoop, its roundness, too great for sight and becoming an emotion,
reducing me to a screaming feeling in the attempt to
articulate it. There was the almost invisible one-manband in his conical brass hat, big drum behind, sticks
strapped to his elbows, clashing cymbals in front, bells on
his feet, possessing the street with his noise. Could that
world—the world of nourishing impressions, the world of
love in the air with mere little white clouds for *pensées*,
of scarlets and sky-blues, or scintillating sky, pounding
sea, fish-flashy rocks, sudden as sickness, the world of
hungry loving people coming and going, infected with
such rapidity, such musical quick speech—could such a
world have stayed, all the 'thought', the cosmetic
emotion, the canned happiness, which have since con-
structed in my distress, would be dismissed. At this time,
too, I had my first love affair, and the most serious and
grand. Next door was a pork-butcher. He slit pigs'
throats in his backyard and let them bleed slowly to
death; they screamed like babies in the night. Out of this
appeared his little daughter, Marie-Thérèse, a solemn
little girl with a ribbon in her bobbed hair, in a pink
frilly dress. I knelt before her and said: '*Marie-Thérèse,
je t'aime.*' She listened, always, but never replied. When
I saw her many years later she was plump for the French
marriage market and more like one's unkindly conception

of a pork-butcher's daughter; perhaps the diet had worked on her. But then too, the heart hadn't a human house, and had eventually to accept its own. But, pulling it clear of all lodgings was, far away, a ghostly mother-hand. She had undoubtedly captured the bird; it danced from twig to twig, and even tried nest-building, till the ghostly wind blew softly and away it went. It was Mother who blew on me.

CHAPTER THREE

On the bright tiles of the *salle à manger* rose, one day, more than six feet of broad M. Joseph, in a big overcoat, grey, over a grey suit, with a brownish face, brown pipe, huge boots, and eyes curiously flat, as though their irises were painted on eggwhite. He was slow; not much happened when he sat, stood, looked; it made me incredibly lively with expectation, and lusty to fill the spaces with sound and action. He was an English Civil Servant on holiday, one-legged and very shy; his hands were huge and hairy with a gold ring and a wrist-watch and walking-stick. At first he always smiled before he spoke, even when he frowned; later, he always made the expression well in advance of the words, so that you knew only too well where you were with him, and craved a little ignorance, which he deemed dishonourable to provide. He looked at me for long periods, making me shift out of his gaze by performing tricks, such as marching in the yard with a tray on my head and distended cheeks in imitation of the one-manband, while he would watch through the glass window. His presence was more than soothing, soporific after the French; I felt drugged and exalted with him, terribly bright, displaying to the maximum. He liked this very much; he took me to Le Touquet where, substantiating his comfortable, easy appearance of having no property-worries, he bought me an unusually expensive tin of sweets to suck while we watched the gallant polo players.

On the beach ('beach' was particularly his word, 'sands' was Mother's) he fanned flat with his stick a space of sand. I took the stick from him and did the same, and he looked displeased, revealing to me that he would need expert ministrations. He bought me a pair of shoes; they gleamed cruelly for Maman was standing by him admiring them with, I'm certain, the sorrow that they were not of her getting, and that I was to wear stranger's things. Then when I put them on the cruelty and rapture continued, and an unreal feeling. His French was hideous but I required him to speak it as I'd forgotten my English, and said I was French. He stayed two weeks and said he'd return. I forgot him.

Life continued evenly for a while after, making ice-cream with Maman, feeding the hens, staring at Grand'-mère. Grand'mère died one night, and I saw her lying in her shiny black coffin with big beautiful silver screws. Her absence thereafter made me a little uncomfortable, the fire having lost its friend; moreover, the old were gentle, not bothered by 'business'. Then, one morning, as I was playing happily in the yard, Maman called me in and I beheld there a Gracious Lady dressed in an elegant blue costume with silver threads, a white fox fur and a picture-hat. 'Ta Maman,' said Madame. 'Non,' I screamed, scurrying to Maman's black skirts, 'Ce n'est pas Maman, t'es Maman.' 'Suis Français.'

A seduction was doubly necessary because Mother was unable to pay a two-years' bill; it started with a scooter the value of which conflicted with that of my hoop; the scooter was fussy, the hoop graceful; the scooter was half-way only to a powered vehicle; I looked anxiously for further conviction that the lady in blue was my mother. She was again living in the rooms by the level-crossing with my sister. And here there came back to me the old aroma of eau-de-Cologne, face-powder, silks, softness everywhere, and Mother's voice which Maman's had never displaced—a 'brown' voice with ripples of silver, which spoke to a place none other could. I began a series of journeys to and fro, feeling frightened but valuable, and displaced. Mother asked whether Madame Tillieux gave me enough to eat? Did she beat me? She said this lovingly anxious for a certain reply which it would have been cruel not to have supplied. Yes, Maman beat me, sometimes, and didn't give me enough to eat—(perhaps I was thinking of the paucity of *gâteaux-bateaux* at this moment, for Maman's food was excellent). I returned to Maman. Later Maman said, had I said these things to Mother? Yes, I had. But was it true? No, I cried. I hurt Maman. But Mother got what she wanted: one day, with no warning to Maman but a letter to arrive later I was whisked off, excited in the conspiracy.

We went to Calais, to an 'Hotel du Port' by the Gare Maritime. The hotel was smelly and dirty, the café part having a zinc and biscuit-coloured bar with a tall, sandy-haired pock-marked lady, standing before the beautiful bottles; her gestures were too anxiously kind to find favour with me; she should have known her pock-marks were unattractive. Her husband was her employee, and seemed only to be 'himself' when he was morosely fishing from the pier. He took me—the second initiation into male sodality—to fish with him; the mood was quiet, womanless, sea-full, with grey sky and wheeling seagulls, the long fishing-line dipping bellying down, and the sodality was almost religious. He was a sad man.

There was more to notice historically at the Hotel du Port. The primary colours were mixing into dirt, the bright people gave away to shaded ones, movements lost briskness in Madame here and the husband; circumstances began to become impermanent. Our room faced the harbour. Beams of the lighthouse at irritatingly regular irregular intervals washed the room in moonlight; Mother slept 'crucified' between my sister and me. It was safe in a precarious world. Below, the café shut late, the sailors were noisy, often fighting, but Mother was our boat. Upstairs was a man who played a concertina; his face was red-hot, and his blue eyes hot, and when I saw him he was eating a piece of raw steak, which he offered me. There was a lot of blood on it and I was frightened, and his face came very near to mine.

The lavatory smelled; I had to pull a handle which depressed a lid at the bottom of the bowl. The café, very noisy at night with drunken sailors, was altogether frightening after the propriety of Maman's teashop; it became terribly important always to be near Mother, who nevertheless was very small and, though almost too brave, often seemed frightened, in the sense of being polite when I knew that naturally she would not have been. And, as she had done once before at Madame Antoine's in Paris, she would appear sometimes, when being polite, to disassociate herself a little from me; I would feel I had become an object if, for instance, she expressed public admiration for me to strangers. I didn't like being noticed when I was with her for it was like leaving her.

One evening we went to a fair among the trees and, as between Maman and the wooden omnibus, I was torn between a bicycle roundabout and Mother, but gave in to Mother. We lived on porridge, curries and *pain d'épice*, a kind of ginger bread; I was terrified of the 'Monkey

Woman', whose monkey pulled my hair out, and who looked like a horrible wicked little man, and whom the ugly Monkey Woman loved, it seemed to me, horribly. Because of the Monkey Woman I was glad to leave the Hotel du Port which we did, I think, after two or three months.

We moved to a small brewery, which we entered through a long stone archway joining two parts of the house, on a cobbled courtyard. The owner was called Adèle, a large and vigorous blonde, her hair swept formidably back to a bun, giving her, with her 'radiant' cheeks (a radiance with a hungry air) a windswept look; her eyes were of that largeness that suggested a challenging ignorance of people which it would have been presumptuous for them to enlighten; for she grew and was great because of what she didn't know, which made the impression of her knowing something better. Her arms were mighty and usually bare to above the sharp elbows. Her husband was a very little Englishman who was obedient and nervous and mousy-coloured with weak, almost tearful eyes; though he didn't intend it, his meek gentleness must have been sensed by her as a terrible accusation; Brunhildes are neurotic. Adèle had a ringing voice, and her husband made 'chuffy' noises, in a high voice become frayed and disconsolate.

We took a small room on the side of the yard opposite Adèle's quarters; I can only remember the bed and the window on its left. Upstairs, regularly at the end of the week, we would hear a man chasing his wife round the table. Once Mother went up, and when she returned she told us he had been chasing her with a carving-knife. Then one day Mother said she must go away again but would return; she left me with my sister.

57

Adèle's vigour put me off and I avoided her—I had always been frightened of shrill voices and a certain kind of misnamed 'vitality', like Jeannette's at Wimereux, which is never content but likes to eat little boys. She appeared to demand some satisfying response from me, which I wouldn't and perhaps couldn't give. It did not seem inappropriate that we began the battle of the faeces. I soon became constipated, and Adèle gave me large enemas—the black tube part had an animate, almost knowing look, and the red bulb looked wicked and powerful. One day after a particularly long bout of wickedness, as she called my constipation (which in her sense it was, because I couldn't relax sufficiently with her to function normally, and hated her from fear) she put me to bed and gave me castor oil. I 'went' uncontrollably in a corner of the room and covered it up with a cloth. She went straight enough up to it as to suggest she'd expected it. She gave a shriek of agonised indignation. It seemed to suit a forming passion that she discovered it, because she thrashed me so hard that the marks were there for two or three days. My sister said in her smallest, neatest voice that I had deserved it because I had been naughty; then I placed my sister with the enemy, who knew what one deserved.

I seemed to be at Adèle's for a very long time. She made me soak beer bottles in buckets of water to take the labels off; the bottles floated oddly to the bottom of the bucket, and I was very content. She took me to see John Barrymore in 'Dr. Jekyll and Mr. Hyde', but told me not to look when the transference scene was showing; but I looked, and for years after had nightmares and made terrible faces to myself in the mirror. She also sent me to a convent, where once they put a dunce's cap on me, because as I can well remember, I had, as so often later, answered some question with no real interest—I have an undirectable 'attention'. But I loved the colonnade, in heavy shadow, in sunlight, round the small playground; I have a fixed image of myself behind a boy trying to pass him to buy sweets from a little stall there. Then one day the big brown M. Joseph came, and I knew him for gentleness. He had a long conversation with the little husband, from which I was only partially excluded. Strangely, when I heard the little husband apologising for Adèle's strong ways I felt sorry for Adèle and even affection for her, and dislike for the little husband and indeed for both men who were speaking against her. I think I saw that Adèle couldn't help herself; her hot eyes revealed a silver thread of 'virtue' quite abstracted from her actions, and this 'virtue' was warmer than the business of the two men. Besides, she was very clean; both men looked a little grubby when they spoke of her. M. Joseph spoke to her, and I think she claimed affection for me. But the enemas stopped, and M. Joseph said he would try to find Mother.

Mother returned and we left. We walked with our belongings—I believe in a pram—for what seemed a long way over the frontier into Belgium, to Furnes. Though I was glad to be with Mother it wasn't a very solid gladness, but relative to a too long absence from her—too long for the link to be remade. There was a hint of politeness in our relations, and of uneven affection in hers, spasmodic in intensity. The room at Furnes was level with the garden and was very damp. At night slugs slid up the walls, and we took turns in keeping awake to knock them down. The landlady was ugly, knobbly, and kind, youngish and tall, and said *Clappemanche* to

me, and *Crollboll*. I sat in a pear tree. Furnes was
dismal in the drizzle; the street near us creaked with a
Singer Sewing Machine sign and advertised a shop full
of wasted, dead sewing machines. Belgium was hotter
in people than France. The men seemed to have too
much blood and an unpleasant liveliness. We were not
long here, and went to Ostend, and crossed to England.

When we were in the train travelling from the English
port to London I noticed an unusual hushedness and
comfort. French trains kick about on the rails and make
noises that prevent one's having the sense of being inside
anything. The carriage is a shell letting everything in.
The English carriage was a moving room, and the material of the passengers' persons closer to the material of
the seats and not utterly distinguished from the thick,
sprung air of the carriage. The passengers were very
oddly at peace, and their 'selves' dwelt a long way back
from their skins and the front of their eyes; the selves
resided in the vehicular body and clothes, whereas in
France they were identical with the vehicle. In England
one had to tap the vehicle or the house to bring the self-
inmate to his ocular windows, where he pulled some
dreamy blind back to look at one. The curtains were of
net, however, and one didn't know how much the abs-
truse calculator was seeing through them. Is life a dream?
I might have thought, had I been older; I felt it was near
to sleep, formally. The knocking of the wheels on the
rails was far away. I had never been so inside anything
before, like a dream. The bus from Waterloo was the
concomitant of the train; we sat sideways on red and
black seats. I spoke rudimentary and guttural English and
the passengers stared at me; I was half frightened and
from fear excited into pleasurable performance. But one

had to gesticulate twice as hard to elicit reactions. The slowness made one's gestures quick-seeming in an air heavier but less substantial. One felt abstractedly quick and thinly blithe, and the performance was exhausting. If the English were not to be stupid they were to be frightening. When we'd alighted in bright and vast Tottenham Court Road the bus rolled off like a little house with its exclusive self-enclosing staircase behind it in a meaningfully private English curve—a curve to be quite a theme of English privacy, seen in mouths and all over the place. The bus was the end of the journey that was the end of France, and we very silently went to Dean Street, which was filthy, into a cellar down smelly curved steps as into some once uninhabited place.

The cellar was two-roomed, the front inhabited one having a big dirty window injecting a feeble light from the area into the room; the area rattled all day long with the sound of people's shoes on the grating.

Here was living Uncle Haslam, who was also Uncle Jacko and Poor Old Bobby Bingo. It is less significant to be striking-looking in England than elsewhere. He was striking-looking; a very long straight nose meeting an out-jutting lower lip above a small chin; a big forehead, a beautifully shaped head, and dark jewelled eyes scanning more 'technically' than intelligently the outer world, capable, in happy moments, of a kind of humour that told one he was at heart almost clear of the performances of human intercourse, as though he'd been a gipsy, or an intelligent Jew; off-setting this was a cravenly pedantic and childish adherence to those performances. Mother made him acutely nervous. He tried to shuffle out of her moral net, getting thereby entangled into docile passivity and even into strained and pathetic admiration. His protests appeared in animal rages. He was a 'character', one who expresses some lost meaning in symbolic ways; the beauty, almost the intellectual beauty, of his face and long lean scholar's body were a tomb to the departed meaning. Mother scribbled on it. She was his punishment; I'd not seen Mother like this before.

He of course believed in his punishment and, in view of his later success, took it as a therapy for adjusting himself to the world; and by means of this objectivity he exploited Mother's naïve bullying—not an uncommon relationship between bully and bullied. Given ever so little confidence he would hold forth in long and longer periods, carefully phrased and of an increasing vulgarity in enjoyment of the mere form. The literary periods reached certain dimensions of inflation and then Mother would prick them, deflate them to some tough little withered rubbery piece of not pretty meaning. Deflated, he was a little boy at school. He was serious, sincere, patient and extremely if narrowly logical; inflated, his sense of grandeur was curiously like Mother's, which explains Mother's generosity. Mother was impressed by his roughest, dimmest logic; her masculine symbol. He was a very dirty man in his cellar, washing out of the saucepan in which he cooked, rarely if ever bathing, wearing stinking socks, but usually appearing above ground in spats, without socks, astonishingly dandified, in city attire, with an oiled manner to correspond with Mother's business one. His dirtiness was in honour of Dr. Johnson, his mentor, after whose cat he named his dog, Hodge. An opera cloak and silk hat were his little bits of the gay past, and a gay wash-drawing of him in evening clothes with the caption: 'Haslam Has a Night

Out'—I think he said by Hablot Brown. I learned later he had been in theatrical circles before his downfall, a friend of Henry Arthur Jones (whom he admired) and member of the Playgoers' Club, to which, at this time, he still rose from the tube station in Tottenham Court Road.

Haslam was not pleased to see me, I thought. He was of the childish order of men who ignore children, lest the dividing rampart fall. For two or three months we lived by day in the cellar and by night at Mrs. Meaty's in Rathbone Place. At around eight o'clock in the cellar I would be placed high on top of the folding bed, Haslam would sit before the Oliver typewriter and business would begin, and continue usually until midnight. Mother was never without a business scheme, each one infallible in its brief life. She thought, for instance, of putting slot-machines in trams, of exporting second-hand typewriters to France, bottles from France to Belgium, of importing manganese through Uncle James in India, while continuing a vague cigarette agency for Teofani in France, and for a wonderful blend called Hadjyani-Vuccino. Jacko met each scheme with elaborately formal scepticism. He would walk up and down aching, as was obvious, for the first declension into conversion; it seemed agreed upon that he should present the kind of obstacles she could best dispose of. Her manner became suave as his ceased to be; she didn't radiate conviction—it was not of that cheap kind: she was a dark well of omniscience forced, by the stupidity of men, to dash token cupfuls of it at them. But in the middle of this she would break off into a small girl's fit of giggling that dismayed Jacko; the perfection of the performance lay in her being able to fall out of it. Living completely on two levels, of hallucinated business acumen and infantile

63

irresponsibility, she was maddening to anyone who took either of them as being exclusive. In later years Jacko almost succeeded in forming his true heart, and this lay in his slowly learning to accept both, and not to point to their mutual incompatibility but suffering the tension himself. Mother dictated, slurring over difficult words and grammatical doubts, at which Jacko took her up like a policeman, pleased as Punch; he was as pedantic as she was inspired. The suave drone of her voice, which I was to hear so often with city friends, was the indication of her slowly leaving reality. Large figures and many capitals of the world loomed up. Business personalities— well-known ones—starred the exciting gloom. This was like a song. In her manner she also affected the complete, fraudulent frankness of business people; an aching frankness, painful to her, of putting 'all her cards on the table', of dramatic, cumulative peaks of 'Look, B., this is abso-lute-ly straight; I believe, candidly, that it's impossible to go wrong. You import so much at . . .' She would dress her face in stiff confessional honour, and seemed unable to transact her business without this expression. Haslam co-operated, like the happy clerk of a prosperous firm. It is odd to reflect that at seven, which I then was, I had a peculiar intuition of their childishness, exacerbated by their insulting exclusion of me; my own omniscience was even then developing competitively.

Their quarrels were terrifying. Mother seemed to undress, or to split down the middle; and from the chasm a strange shriek would proceed; Jacko would growl and then roar like an animal. Grey-faced, he would stalk up to the place where his many curved pipes were kept, select one with convulsive discrimination and, with a timed yelp, break it. He would then hiss between

clenched teeth: 'Got the lot! Got the bloody lot!' or
'Poor old Bingo, poor old bloody old Bobby Bingo'.
Mother's voice would become icy, exact, her expression
deadly aloof and terribly 'pure' and holy. 'I cannot
stand another moment, Bobby. I cannot stand it!' And
she would go, my heart racing. Once she said she was
going to drown herself from the embankment; a constable was sent after her, and both returned respectably.

Haslam had knobkerries, Mother always carried a
police-whistle and loved to say 'Constable, can you
direct me to . . .' They liked her. We lived mainly on
Heinz Tomato Soup and Pritchard's sandwiches. At
midnight I would be awakened from an uncomfortable
doze and trotted over to Mrs. Meaty's, where much of
the night was spent in hunting and squashing bugs—
Mother would only point them out to us, never squash
them. At Mrs. Meaty's in the morning Mother began to
beat my sister with the back of a brush, a punishment
my sister passed on to me with her hand on my head. I
remember once pleading for my sister—I was very
frightened of violence—but found her unappreciative
and even insulting. They were more together than
Mother and myself; our relationship was convulsive and
unreal. In a tittery way, also, they thought males comical,
which shamed me.

We were sent to the convent in Leicester Square for a
while. I took a fearful dislike to the nuns. They were
white, lineny and mechanical; their punishments were
cruelly abstract and ruthless; they would make the children kneel in a row and, if they wept sufficiently, they
were not sent to the 'coal-cellar' whither they'd been
condemned. They rapped our hands sharply and surprisingly with a ruler; their smiles were to me frighteningly

'technical', a pale mouth separating for the display of square white teeth; their eyes strangely dead, but with an odd bright light. I always breathed prayers, and felt an emptying of stomach-consciousness close to fainting which still recurs occasionally in similar circumstances. To offset the nuns I would hear 'Yes we have no bananas' and 'Sheik of Araby' played in the mornings in Dean Street on a lazy-strung barrel-organ; there were also oval pewter milkcans, and Mother, her scent; coffee and silks.

I could not understand why life was emotionally colder here, so much more so, than it had been at Madame Tillieux'; I felt cut off from the flesh of humanity, defined too distinctly as an individual; children secretly like to be anonymous, a part of something greater, but they nervously co-operate with misguided adults in the opposite process of identifying themselves with imposed individualism; it is this that makes for precocity.

Far away in Bombay were Grandmother, who three times sent Mother the fare to come out in vain; Uncle James, tea-planting and also in touch with us; and my father's family whom we never saw.

I was now seven, and feel, thirty years later, little changed; the personality forming round the child is as bleak as it is versatile; its accomplishments in displaying all the *simulâcra* of the real, which means unhappily the childish, destroys true childishness. Presumably one forgets. I was already 'escapist' and preferred strangers to intimates and foreign places to familiar ones. Silence, solitude, began with an internal babble. But when that had finished there'd be something menacing or something mysteriously sad about the so important objects around me. They had a dull, deadening language to

speak, a paralysing truth to tell: as though the truth of
the world were held by objects not by people, as though
they were of greater importance: things began their army
organisation into existence, and would steadily encroach
and animate, like Frankenstein's monsters in furniture.
This experience made me feel seriously lacking in
identity, which seemingly depended upon the demar-
cating presences of other people. I was—and am—like a
cup of water without the cup, and dangerously flowed
into other people's ways of being, sometimes requiring
the impossibility of real fusion to reach a crisis before I
could be brought to bring me back to some desert island
with a rag flapping for flag on it, myself. I was cruel to
people as a rudimentary means of preventing myself
from becoming identified with them.

Because Mother and I had never developed our
relationship its quality became one of esoteric intimacy,
crazily different from my relationship with others; when
she went, I divided and consulted myself, the substitute
for her, and lavished upon myself the tenderness she
would have lavished upon me. She and I lived in a dark
cave of fearful cosiness, which fresh air would destroy, in
which the sounds and movements of others are hideous.

It is a sad day when one realises, partially, that the
envied organic quality of other people's identities can't
be for oneself, and that one's natural silly little over-
simple ways must be acknowledged as eccentricity, like
Uncle Haslam's behaviour. This is the hardening-up of
unemployable conditions of childhood, which a gap in
development kept in an unhealthy fluidity for too long.

The parent regards the child with metaphysical love-
hungry eyes, and especially did so thirty years ago; the
little Eldorado of his heart was being mined. Children

are too often believed to have in their souls, or hearts or what you will the panacea for mature evils; in excessive instances of this regard from parents, children may be made mad with unconscious terror out of the sheer exhaustion of the relationship.

The wish to be a child again was common after the 1914–18 war; understandably; and fruitful of elaborate whimsies. With the Germans it took the form of wishing to be children dressed in big men's clothes. Parents wanted their children to give them the key to the door of their gone childhoods: the result, a precocity from the children, neurotic, formalistic and starved. The children became little parents, and parenthood became thinly technical. When Mother placed on me and drove into me her soul-suffused eyes, their large animal hearts pulling for sustenance and particularly for forgiveness about a guilt evident in her on my account, my reaction was supra-objective. I blithely dismissed her demands that I should feel life to be nothing without her.

The transference to my prospective guardian was arranged one evening in the basement; I later understood that M. Joseph, as I'd known him, after leaving Adèle's in Calais had traced Mother and asked her to let him look after me. She had agreed. So, all of the other world, he appeared in our cellar; the texture of his tweed coat was composed of clean grey and silver threads; his size thirteen boots shone. He appeared gloriously clean and fresh in our cellar, and he looked very affectionately at me, and spoke to Mother with a queer caution, 'dealing with' her. Uncle Haslam was making many more coughs than usual, clearing his throat for some of his most affable, cordial, businesslike expressions; he looked winningly at my guardian, who evidently felt suddenly odd in our set-up. Indeed, Uncle Haslam was beside himself to agree with my guardian, his voice slurring into those queer business tones I'd come to know so well, like cars with sweet engines driving away on a fair road. My guardian liked Uncle Haslam, and I saw they were pleased to be men together, and were very reasonably ever so subtly, in a way directed against my dark-eyed, crumpled Mother. My Mother was losing me, leaving me again, and she sat on a chair beside the doorway leading upstairs to the street, against the wall. Her eyes now had a trance-like steadiness, their pupils glowing, but with their points of concentration seeming to recede back into her unconscious; she must have been sipping at what she assumed to be the cup of her fate. Mothers losing their children look unconscious as mothers meeting their children look brilliant. I, the object, emotionally crept away from her on all fours, hoping she'd not notice the emotional unplugging. My manner I kept affectionate in ways that faltered as I felt the growth of my impatience to be gone on the nice new vehicle, my guardian. But I didn't want to show this; my tones were low and faltering; and I had the impression she didn't notice my behaviour, or even, scarcely, myself. It was an idea, familiar to her, that I would go. She looked like a Madonna dragged through the world. Her eyebrows were very level and beneath them and above her eyes, under the bone, the slight arch of beauty. Then my guardian went out and returned with some Wellingtons he'd bought me to take to his hut. She looked a victim, a sacrifice, and Uncle Haslam a volubly self-selling person who nevertheless felt for her under his glibness; but my guardian didn't. No, he came for his pound of flesh, all living, to comfort him; 'emotionally deprived', he wanted sustenance; something, as we say, to 'lavish his love upon'; the lavishee wanted some Wellingtons. I can think of Mother's consciousness at that time as a deep well receiving a stone, and waiting for it in her heart's ear to sound the lonely and desolating 'tock', faintly and fatally, on the bottom.

My kiss for her was of the briefest; hers for me horrible to remember—wet. She cried slowly, and I went rapidly. My guardian and I stayed in an hotel that night to leave next morning for his hut on the hill.

CHAPTER FOUR

I was exhilarated at leaving Mother; many changes had given change a dreamy normality in which I could be more myself while I was diminished and depersonalised by threats of permanence. I was, moreover, unused to the company of men, and was pleased with the extra resonance of what I said to them, which included many things—I didn't know why—that I was unable to say to women: perhaps a co-operative mental adventure that women, aware of the fundamental risks, are less willing to share. I felt I could say anything to Uncle C.

I emerged from the Dean Street cellar relieved at once of a gathering bric-à-brac of confusion; my freedom was intoxicating. Uncle Joseph held my hand and I became conscious of his soft pads linked with mine. The brightest bus took us to Charing Cross Station; I listened appreciatively to its loud purring and inhaled its delicious petrol fumes. I relished the assurance, a meal of confidence to me, with which he so methodically and evenly bought the tickets, not hurrying panicked to his trouser pocket as Mother did to her silver-chained bag, none of us sure of what she'd find there, but holding his money without attachment certain it was there and wouldn't run away. He was incapable of having holes in his money pocket. Money obviously came to him on an evenly working conveyor belt, as long as society, whereas with Mother money erupted discordantly like squibs

71

round her feet, and she had to dart and pray to get any. Moreover he didn't shriek *Combien?* with a tragic moan, as Mother did; but having been told the price, quite coolly paid it. I sensed his power, and thrilled to it.

The train was his servant, a chain of mild carriages waiting for *us*; it slowly moved off, it slowly gathered speed, it sweetly sang its rhythmical melodies; it gently put to sleep my essentially economic terrors, and turned my guardian into a monument, ready for my future blasting operations. The orderly landscape with its little trees, little houses and little stations with neat little people on them, which later became as dull as Haydn's umpteenth symphony, was to me then the whole of human benevolence. It was a crinolined chorus of security, sobriety, sweetness and normality. Strange how I later turned round and went for it like a mad dog, and how, recently, since it has acquired something of my old insecurity, I have discovered in myself a little of its old peace.

Big green banks came to a halt as our journey ended. I saw the old porter ramble forward and salute my guardian intimately; he was a 'comfortable', grey, dingy man, as English as teacups held by people on blue-flowered carpets near a bay window. He slightly chilled me.

The station was very quiet once the train had gone, as we waited to cross the rails. It was evening, bluish, a little raw, a little damp, like all Surrey. We clambered up to the miniature railroad in the chalk-works, which extended to the foot of our hill. Then, in motion again, happiness came back; standing still with him was going to be irritating—his personality was rather squeezing. His big brownish face turned suddenly to me was a shock of childishness, of big space unmatured with meaning, like fields unploughed, the eyes not, unhappily, more than big white boils with brown in the centre— mono-expressive. Emotions would be a colic with him. We cheerily, like comrades, moved over the chalk-works, myself thoroughly in with him in our conspiracy of living alone together for ever. He hopped in his walk, his artificial leg slightly thrown forward on the supports of his 'good' leg and walking-stick, which darted out like a magician's wand; his overcoat was very big and sailed gallantly out. He was very swift in his hopping walk, and very clever at surmounting the slippery chalk path at the beginning of the hill. It was darker at the top of this; he flashed his torch on and dived, myself behind, into an overgrown copse with a soft leaf-covered floor, wherein was thick silence; we emerged on to a plateau a little way up the hill, and here he turned with authoritative contemplation to the lines of car lights below and the twinkling lights of the distant towns and villages above which we characteristically found ourselves. He mopped his brow with an open affection for it, grinning with pleasure at being able to like himself with someone else watching; the silence was bewitching, grandiosely ornamental to our outlined, heroically definitive shapes and persons. 'Won't be long,' he said, as we dived off again under the high disused railway bridge, his stick slightly tocking in echo. We followed the vaguely visible white path, then sharply to the right up the steep part of the hill. Half-way up he stopped, sat down, and brought out his pipe, which he filled with the stuff whose smell I learned to love as being the harbinger of his good moods—actually Lloyd's Skipper Navy Cut, a taste for which I inherited from him along with the rusty iron hook of his British conscience— in revenge, I suppose, for my desertion. He smoked with immense satisfaction, his cod-shaped mouth curled as much as it could with something as near to lasciviousness as he could sustain. He blew the smoke out in big clouds, anointing the air; then, he became a big man-engine for me, like a locomotive, the smoke another sign of his power. It was good to be small with such a big man. He liked adventures with guaranteed harbours.

The valley, the lights, the car sounds were falling away from us, as we rose, our hearts stimulated by climbing, into the night sky; on the brow of this gathered the suggestion and dim picture of a shrine for our dwelling, a place alone, high—and—yes—religious. It was; a little wooden shack twelve feet by eight. He unlocked the wooden door, we climbed up three wooden steps, and by the torchlight I saw dusky shapes, a cupboard opposite the door and a table and chairs. He shone his torch on St. Anthony in a cassock with a red poppy on him in a specially made niche in the far corner. St. Anthony, a sort of bachelor's guardian, would look after us; my guardian was a militant atheist, but was friendly to ascetic, and perhaps misogynistic saints. We went to bed, he in an army stretcher and I in his metal bed.

In the morning at once my education away from the past began with him, and from then until my sixteenth year he instilled into me his major discovery, wrested out of attempted seductions into other faiths—that a spade was a spade. Nothing have I more bitterly resented than this so-called 'fact', the truth of which exists only in the face of colossal opposition. To live, I would think, in a country where this passes for thought, for morality, for science maybe . . . yet, it was a major discovery for many at this time. My new adjustment to phenomena—a tin of condensed milk for instance—began thus: he takes a tin of Nestlés milk from the cupboard, which he can reach without rising from the stretcher. 'Milk,' he says, with the onomatopœic succinctness of Mr. Squeers, 'thick rich milk. This'll do you good. Get some hot tea with this in it in your inside and you'll feel all right. Cup of cha in the morning.' He puts rashers of bacon in the frying-pan and, with some fumbling, lights the oil-stove (he would not then or after have truck with primuses); smells and crackling and the hot 'cha' steaming, soon the little wooden hut filled with it. He hands me mine (excellent bacon he always bought, pink and white) and we eat; as he eats, his face gets a little pinkish under his yellowish complexion, and his eyes moisten. He eats as though he were being nourished on the spot, and beams like an advertisement sun at the end; that is, after 'Keiller's Marmalade, thick, chunky, bitter'—'I like a thick marmalade, bitter'. Then the pipe. Smoking, he talks—and I can never remember what other people say, having always been more concerned with what I would say when they stopped. He must have said what he said later, though—I doubt if he ever said anything merely once. That might be, 'No frills and fancy stuff here, m'boy: hard, plain stuff, good substantial food—sleep hard, rise early'—(he dawdled till ten or eleven whenever he could in bed)—'fresh air, exercise—like the Army. I built this meself. Wonderful little hut it is too; stands up to any weather; must creosote it again when the warm weather comes. Best matchboarding inside.' He looks round smirking, delighted with himself for being in the hut, he 'made'—or rather, fitted together from prefabricated sections. He is amazingly delighted with himself at everything he does. He hadn't expected, I suppose, he could do anything.

It was his face I first remember disliking. It was pudding, with implements of physical needs stuck on it, and in the ugly kind of coy functionalism early engineering displays. Its greatest tedium lay in the arched and permanently-raised eyebrows, giving him an expression of continuous and unfruitful astonishment; everything I said and did appeared to surprise him, till I became a wonder. At first this delighted me; every word was expelled on a bundle of compressed air with a little ping at the release which was like a shot in the arm for self-wonder. For any droll action I was made to feel the author of a fireworks display; I had accidentally set our relationship off on just the right foot when I had marched with a tray on my head for his amusement at Wimereux. But the novelty of purchasing his admiration wore off; moreover, if I could feed his insatiable appetite for sweetmeats *à l'humaine* I could also stick little pins into his vast unconscious expanses, for instance by openly registering disgust as he murdered apples with abominable salivatory noises in his big many-toothed mouth. His slowness, formerly an emblem of my security, was a more inevitable target; he would grow infuriated if I finished sentences for him, while to wait was impossible—I simply felt I was disappearing as I listened. There would be a regular sequence involving a grimace (a sweet smile rubbed out with a wry one), a cough, a shift of the body, and finally the dim damp words, hearses dressed in mourning, evidently, for the death of their meaning obscured in the coffin. But, he was kind—extremely; and, to my horror, extremely sensitive—probably more so than myself. For many years I learned not to hurt him, and winced vilely when anyone else did so unwittingly. Furthermore he was good, he was honest; in a simplicity beyond so many, he wanted to know, to understand, and then to act upon his understanding. And he was brave; his sense of right was impermeable granite, and much of my easy virtue still litters his rocks. For this quality of honesty, which my mother had spiritualised for purely transcendental traffic, I loved him passionately, for nothing is more lovable than honesty.

His aesthetic folly lay in his lower middle-class roots, perhaps in his deracination from working-class ones that lay recently behind him. He seemed to be experiencing emotions of a novel complexity for which his machinery of expression was completely inadequate; hence his awkwardness, his shyness, hums and hahs, and downright ugly smirks, and intense self-apology smeared thinly on silly conceit; hence the outstanding skeletal monster of him and his type—the doggy egalitarianism, the resentment at life immorally untrammelled; the dreadful, vile, vulgar thought resident in its cranium, souring its heart. Being of another type, I embarrassed him until I learned to adopt his methods and inelegant inarticulacy, and to adopt his notion that the dumb was the good because the bad had the habit of being the articulate: an understandable prejudice, but dangerous because it is used effectively against the application of the good and apparently justifies that over-simplification of human adventure into the exclusively moral dimensions of Heaven and Hell.

Uncle Joseph was on holiday in his hut and before long we returned to London, taking rooms at 37, Batis Street near Clapham Common, let by a Mrs. Law, wife of an Australian waiter. Precociously aware of people's characteristics, it was the driven drone of Mrs. Law's voice that I picked on to rationalise my dislike; it was a kind of ugh-ugh sound which overrode the sense of her words as compulsively as the tube train noise; it is this ugh-ugh sound which in its varying inflection and intensity reveals the underlying attitudes of the various strata of English middle-class society. Mrs. Law's particular brand had something of her class 'moral motor-horn' in it, and it aggravated me the more intensely because of the contrast with French *brio* and conciseness which still relieves me when I hear it. She received me into her arms with an ecstasy that ensured the development of my exclusiveness already latent within me—a characteristic most unpopular in an 'equality' as formal as ours.

Her husband, Lawdy, as she called him, was extremely tall and well-built and difficult to imagine constricted in a waiter's duties and clothes; he had developed a sneer as a defence against the crushing of those Australian gaucheries which his wife stamped on in the ardour of her suburbanity; otherwise she adored him uncritically, and he, sensing that a more discriminating affection would be more bearable, delighted sometimes to spill the ubiquitous connubial soup. Another three-cornered division developed, and I took his side because he liked me, because I was beginning automatically to side with men against women and because I sympathised with his sneer—a backdoor art to self-respect I had already learnt from my guardian.

My power of detached observation, or perhaps revulsion of physical coldness, bred in me a general contempt in which I myself was not at that time included; however, it enabled me to discover the techniques of expression in

78

different classes, professions and individuals. My cross-social-breeding had ill-equipped me for the adoption of a typical class-tone; I was therefore delighted when I read Dickens to read his consciousness of the various modes, while feeling in their shell of mannerism the hungry vampire for community that lay in himself; for the excess of this kind of definition lies in missing the so organic unity of individual and type, individual being at the base of the cone. Prospective permutations of class and professional manners, grasped intuitively by prospective virtuosi, account for a great deal of sexual attraction—indeed they are the surface-sucking antennae in the game.

We had not long been here when my guardian chose a school for me; a dingily select establishment called Eton House School and run by a Miss Bancroft for the more refined children of a district the self-elevation of which was revealed in the nasal pronunciation of its inhabitants. I came most immediately under the supervision of Miss Bancroft—a more severe version of Miss Pipchin. Her face, like so many faces I was now encountering, consisted chiefly of flexible furniture for the expression of public emotions, or a reverent self-arrangement of the draperies of old yellow soul-skin; when she suddenly lifted these draperies round her mouth, I was frightened, unless I saw that she had determined upon a smile which she would then execute ruthlessly. Her false teeth were large and bluish white, and when she opened her mouth the effect was like that of the sudden self-opening of a piano lid, for a moment. She was tall, straight and thin, dressed in grey and mauve woollens with a long string of tooth-like beads round her functional neck; her head being capped with a dusty hat of grey hair. Her shoes were extraordinarily long, jutting inward to sharp points at the toe-joints like an old crone's jawbone but flat, and turned severely outwards from the ankle as though in hospitality to the space ahead. The legs rising from them—that is, the decent few inches visible—were tubular, in light grey woollen stockings. Sage grey eyes flickered uncapturably behind her pince-nez which rode a formidable nose; the pince-nez concealed the eyes less than that look of skill in dealing with people—a look that says that it knows enough to dispense with seeing anything at all. You met curtains when you looked her in the eye, and felt foolish for expecting something else, for decent people don't have eyes to be looked into, any more than they travel in the nude. Her face was so much like a window that a fantastic effect was achieved when she spied through the genuine window of her kitchen on to us children in the playground. She liked me, so that automatically I disliked her to the extent of exposing my most tender and abject charms. She saw docility and an angel expression; women without love can be deceived. I dreaded the first day, and in fact arrived at the wrong school, one for girls higher up the hill. Once in class, however, I enjoyed the obvious opportunities for displaying my skill in the things I liked—such as reading; I went mad with impatience while others read, imagining as I listened to them my own superb execution, for I loved the sound of my voice. I liked history, identifying myself at once with all kings, having been brought up to consider myself the heir to the Irish throne; as this ideal identification didn't work, I soon chose the inversion of it, Christ.

But I didn't fit in; the mutedness that had so impressed me on arrival in England was developing into an awareness of what foreigners call, rightly or wrongly,

English Hypocrisy. There was a dearth of immediate and unsifted response to me; diplomacy began so young, and the wall of nervous, pernickety tabus was used as a filter for all reactions. The children were almost little institutions, little snippets of ideology. Their moral 'Oooo's' and 'Aaaah's' made me groan, their legalistic little minds, which sped them off to tell some wretched authority about every mishap, their dingy volubility about what was 'fair' and what wasn't, their shouting declarations of their 'rights'—all these things, like civilisation itself, depressed me. For one sensed the shaking little jelloid personality behind these fire-curtains. No wonder they hero-worshipped opposite personalities lacking inhibitions, and even criminals, for those who practise ideals have some feeling for their own health. Then, of all paradoxes, their immense, pompous egotism took the form of the most complacent and lying modesty I'd encountered; they behaved as the tremendously privileged sharers, or slices of, one big national ego. They were little slices of one big Mother Spam who hung in the air—or fog rather. The only way I could make any contact, therefore, was by sharp methods. I began with one little boy with the unbelievable name of Donald Darling, who appeared to me to have the unpleasant aspect of combined milk and urine in his face—or was it rather that he smelt of urine? Him I systematically pinched, aided by my lieutenant, Allen. We pinched him as epicures of cruelty, having a sip now and then, as it were. He complained of course, and there was quite a pother from his parents, but I was so gentle in my manner that I think it must have been very difficult for the teacher to believe me capable of such things. When the logic of the situation demanded, I would decide automatically to look innocent, and in order to do so I would simply make myself feel it like a sincere actor; but this does not mean that there is any connection between a child's real self and his good self demanded by the bullyings of his 'loving' elders. The ready-made portrait of the good self can be held up whenever required, and the more practice his elders give him the less it means to the child to hold it up; moreover, he'll sometimes make eyeholes in the portrait and stare through it at his dumb elders disturbingly. If we ask for an advertisement of moral perfection we'll get it.

I was not as good an actor as some, however, perhaps because I had a dawning awareness of its 'duplicity'; yet I could not regard the act as wholly unworthy, for sometimes my affection demanded it in order to conceal my more critical intelligence. Affection's contempt for intelligence is well known, the British heart being the solvent of the British brain.

At my most relaxed I sat, wonderfully unself-doubting, absolute, controlled, on a throne in me from which I could afford to laugh at the tensions of 'leadership' trembling in the faces of amateurs at the game. At such times my face wore the forms of the family infallibility, and with this I would stand on a bench in the playground and conduct the skipping of the little girls. I would bark tersely, with few encouraging smiles; I was thrilled with their obedience, though they tended to show they needn't obey if they didn't want to—a bit of nonsense I could later ascribe to vulgar egalitarianism. I was disgusted with the aching and panting subservience of the little servant-children to this ideal and was incapable of taking adult commands seriously. And this natural inability to obey was heightened because to do so

would have been to divide myself in my loyalty to my
guardian who consulted me like a grown-up, explained
everything so that unavoidably we were in league against
other grown-ups who didn't—those who blew trumpets
at children.

But the growing limitations and inefficacy of my
earthly rule soon made me turn to transcendental
territories. I entered the spirit world, like a Bayswater
medium. I told my lieutenant one day of his destiny to be
my high-priest, my religious agent. We did our gym in a
drill-hall close by, and one day, while watching the cudgel-
play of the older girls which they did in their blue
knickers (perhaps a springboard to the transcendental)
I was seized with trembling excitement. I observed the
activities cautiously, made sure no one was noticing me,
and said to Allen: 'Say nothing—don't look—I'll show
you a devil under a loose block over there.' He nodded, I
then said—'Say nothing, tell no one—you promise?'
He did; 'Then, a few days ago, when the sun was shining,
I found myself slowly going to heaven. I went up and up
and up and up. And there at the top I met God, and he
told me I must go down again and tell him what was
happening down here. I met also Jesus Christ. So we
must watch out, and I'll show you where the devil's hid.'
His fishy eyes behind his glasses looked as sensible as
before, and I took care to believe he believed me. My
eyes were wet with spiritual uplift, and my voice was
finely wavering, modelled on a priest's. Then, when he
was invited to a party without me, I warned him in the
shaking voice not to go because, I promised him, abund-
ant devils would be present. 'I know', he said, 'but I can
manage them.' 'You can't without me,' I said. 'It's a big
risk.' 'No,' he said, 'I can manage them. I'd better go to

see what they are anyway.' I suspected him of hypocrisy but couldn't objectify my own enough to accuse him of it—that would have brought our church down. I swallowed defeat.

Thus began the consciousness of my divinity, and when, years later, I met in Soho the pathological pretender to an extinct throne my eyes watered with fellow-feeling for this fellow-hero in delusion, because I at once knew its sad origin—of loneliness which sang out of his tones, and which he ignored, having royalty enamelled completely over his mind.

This consciousness of my divinity may have sprung from a family characteristic, for we had an aunt in Spain whose religious mania led her to spread newspapers on the floor by her bed to sleep on, and though Mother giggled at this extremity of self-mortification, she had enough of the same quality to pass it on to me, and it developed in me along a logical path to its explosion. Ethically it had a long life, tagging on to theories of the infallibility of the deep inner self, in D. H. Lawrence, and the whole school of intuitive popes in literature; but in childhood it served another purpose; it allowed me to reject the logical inference that being different from the others by reason of my different background and experience was wicked, and it helped me to resist the feelings of guilt which monsters were trying to induce in me, impelling me to confessions of crime. On great days the sense of rightness was the heart expanding like a tulip to the heavens from which divine justification poured; we rejected the blackmail of identification into the miserable technological age, and said the true self was at the receiving end of divine communication.

Divinity and happiness, or love, motivated my first

crime; lack of money made it possible. The stages were: lack of money, fear, love, divinity, theft. I had become very fond of a little girl with straight-bobbed hair and tilted brown eyes, Chinese-fashion, nimbler and gayer than the general pudding. One day I found I was without my customary twopence, and through association with early family circumstances I was filled with terror. Fear turned, when they'd all gone out of the classroom, to beatitude; I felt light and whimsical, but also purposeful and clear-headed as I opened the brown lid of her desk and in sugar-tong fingers picked out two pennies, whose round brownness still look awful to me. Breathless I descended to the place where milk and biscuit were distributed, waiting with panting heart for my name to be called. When it came, with a frightfully unnecessary chattiness I paid the twopence and took the milk; the gauze curtains of Miss Bancroft's eyes seemed, for a second, to twitch aside to allow her blue hatchet-shaped monsters to scald my eyes. The room became much thinner, the objects more substantial, menacing, and the milk completely tasteless, the biscuit undesirable. There seemed a silent noise of staring objects circled round me, there was a silence in the flabby sun that shone through the classroom window and the dust was immobile; the large nicer motherly teacher wore her face with the greatest care I'd ever seen, in case a bit of justice be spilled off by its movement; 'Connie has missed two pennies from her desk which were there this morning'; her jaw moved in and out in a steady rhythm, 'If anyone knows anything about this will he or she please own up?' I sat steady, my shoulders like a coathanger to my suspended body, and said nothing. Then the fever of fear and guilt mounted and, later, trembling, white and sweaty, I owned up. I was taken out into the cold hall of the school, or rather the passage to the street, to confront Miss Bancroft and the nicer teacher seated side by side on a bench. Miss Bancroft looked thoroughly dead and stupid. She wagged her voice and said with extreme vulgarity that people went to prison for stealing; so, having established in my mind no connection between going to prison and being wicked, my ethical standards already being developed beyond that, she was unable to forgive me. For the next few days I felt spiritual distinction and earthly humiliation as an outcast. The little girl, her vivacious face gone puddingy, her lively eyes turned to bloated little brown stomachs, would not speak to me. Frankly, I regarded this as rank hypocrisy; I could not see her behaviour at all conforming to her nature. So, I went 'within' a little more. I knew without doubt I'd stolen 'communicatively' and happily; and that the results were excommunicative.

CHAPTER FIVE

U ncle Haslam had been alone for several months
now, Mother being in France engaged in further
business, with my sister. In this temporary freedom whose end he dreadfully expected at any moment he
had, at first hesitantly, blossomed. First he had returned
to his first love, drink; but in a surprisingly controlled
way. Secondly, with the courage of what Mother called
his imbecility, his complete lack of business understanding, his inability to 'Write a decent letter' and to deal
with people, he had become manager of a large marble
works in Kennington, on the verge of Walworth, where
also he had taken a flat. Thus established, elements of a
friskiness, not at all evident under Mother's regime, re-
appeared; and an intellect engaged in what Mother called
Bilge—the study of Dr. Johnson, history, poetry. Uncle
Haslam had once, I later learned, been a 'character' in
the early nineteen hundreds. With a new red tip to his
tremendously long straight nose he returned, in a sadly
diminished way, to these interests. Kennington and the
marble works, however—and time also—had reduced
the 'character' into an eccentric. My guardian and I
sometimes visited him, usually on a Sunday. We would
arrive about eleven, climb the dirty staircase and go to
his front room, where we would find him surrounded
with his stacks of old books, mainly eighteenth-century
volumes of obscure poets and novelists, his Egyptian

mummy-head in its case, his knobkerries and array of enormous pipes, and inevitably, on the mantelpiece, a bottle of Tarragona. My guardian and he would sample this while he gingerly prepared the joint for entry into the oven. He would turn the gas very low, with immense satisfaction—he was doing everything Mother said he couldn't do—explain that the art of good cooking consisted in slow cooking (in the two hours of 'opening time' on Sundays), garland the joint with potatoes and, at twelve, set out for the local while I wandered around the flat or went out for a walk.

With my guardian he was conspiratorial against my Mother, women had no sense of proportion, they were excitable, melodramatic, they 'squawked', he said, at every opportunity, and took pleasure in killing peace. 'Look at us now,' he would roughly say; 'the joint sizzling in the oven—the potatoes hissing, going a soft gold-brown; our glasses of Tarragona full, our pipes on fire, the clock gently ticking—Sunday mid-day—what more could a man want? Bring a woman in—rush— joint burning, potatoes dry—get out of my way, nuisance —screams, tears, things upset. Why? Such is woman's nature.' He professed a surprising scepticism of Mother's business abilities—schemes, as they were called in the family—which made me recall the devotedly impressed way he had listened to her in Dean Street, as he did until she died. He said I was the best of the family, seemingly balanced. He approved of my guardian; they liked each other, Uncle Haslam slightly envious of my guardian's security, my guardian of Uncle Haslam's 'character' and intellect (I found no evidence of that, though Mother had said he was a very clever man). I became aware now of Uncle Haslam's fine-shaped head, perfect egg-shaped,

with crisp black curls round the back of a receding hair-
line; beetle-brows, with odd hairs descending over his
eyes; eyes gold-flecked brown, of a terribly humorous
intelligence; his very long straight nose; a brief upper lip
slammed tight on a jutting lower one, and a small sharp
chin; teeth yellow and projecting, like dogs'. To complete his profile was usually one of his big-bowled pipes
with a long curved stem.

Details of his past appeared; he had begun practising
for law, after having started as an art-master (he had
some talent for ink line drawings), when Mother invaded
him in his chambers in the Temple and made things
impossible, I gather. He had written a book: a handbook
on Port Sunlight, for Lever Brothers. He was a staunch
Conservative and Royalist, in an eighteenth-century
way from—despite his incredibly filthy person (which
changed in Kennington)—his love of order, ritual and
precedence in social life. His God was Dr. Johnson, and
Gray one of his favourite poets; later, under Mother's
romantic influence, he became an Edgar Wallace fan. I
discovered years later from a City acquaintance of his
that he had two reputations: as a wit, and as the soul of
honesty. He was, definitely, an incorruptibly honourable
man, and terribly shocked often by Mother's business
casuistry. Of his wit I have little evidence.

He took us round the marble works, explaining in great
detail the different kinds of stone; while he was doing this
I stole his fountain-pen. A little later he gave me a half-
crown to buy him something which fell down the drain
as I rolled it along the pavement. I was acutely embarrassed in telling him what had happened, for, though
he accepted the story, it seemed to me entirely inadequate; it seemed reasonable to be suspected of stealing

the half-crown despite his ignorance of my stealing the pen.

Some months later we called on him again; the transformation was complete. Mother had returned, thrown all his dirty clothes, shirts, opera-hat and cloak, books and knobkerries into the smallest back room; the Egyptian lady stared from below the cistern in the lavatory. He was wretched-looking, spoke jerkily, his eyes hardly visible under his overhanging eyebrows, and rigid in a fate-haunted expression. He was unshaven, sallow and dirty, and soon dived into his kennel. Later in the afternoon when the others were in the front room he asked me through the door in a whisper to come in; in the greying light I saw the horrible squalor of the place—dirty laundry and so forth everywhere; he was lying on his back on the bed, one leg stiff in the air, and when I asked him what he wanted, he continued what evidently had been a long recitation: 'The ploughman homeward plods his weary way, And leaves the world to darkness *and to me.*' At 'me' he stopped dramatically, and gave me a fixed look. Would I bring him, without telling Mother, a glass of Tarragona from the bottle on the kitchen mantelpiece? I did so with swimming eyes. In front, Mother had explained that he was not fit to live anywhere but in a pigsty, where she'd installed him; my childish mind wondered: the flat had been remarkably clean before. From that time forward Uncle Haslam's decline continued to her death. Living with her he lost his will, his 'ability' to work, everything pertaining to survival. At her death he was again resurrected: with a certain loss in delicacy, and a gain in effectual vulgarity.

Uncle Haslam played a part in my guardian's developing propaganda against Mother, substantiating some of the things he said. It was certainly true that behind his back she laughed at all the qualities in him that, later, I was to find so depressing—his slowness of mind and body, his little conceits: she was also vilely snobbish about him. One of his names being Camden, she liked to call him (a good specimen of Mother's wit) 'Camiknickers'; usually when she met him she borrowed five pounds.

I was now truly 'settling down' with my guardian, passionately loving him, boasting of his prowess, powers and intellect to everyone. I wanted to be with him alone. He was as shy as myself, and along with other reasons this was to hasten our departure for the hut again, already our implicit desire. All this indicates the development of my introversion—a hackneyed term used to put an experience more sympathetically seen as mental pioneering into a category of fruitlessness; it seemed fruitless because my ideas outstripped and therefore became more important than my ability to verbalise them. But I found supporters of my mental endeavours in books and films; my greatest supporter was Chaplin. My guardian took me to see *The Kid* and *The Goldrush* at the Shakespeare Cinema, a delightful old theatre, musty, huge ornamental plush and gold. In *The Goldrush* I remember squealing orgastically with excitement and crying and laughing simultaneously. He was sensible, though funny, two qualities for me, only obsessionally identified. More directly and vividly than any other, he justified my ways because he showed how sensible, logical behaviour led to confusion, how simple people get into a mess and how scoundrels have the best haircuts and incomes. I intuitively disagreed that the sensible straightforward actions such as Chaplin's should be 'funny', whereas crooked complex ones, such as the morons' in other

American films, should be 'sensible' and that the converse was a proper indication of a tragically cruel and stupid world. I had never known such love for, and such excitement about, someone I didn't know personally; that tears and laughter should be so utterly combined overpowered me. I vaguely glimpsed that this meant 'all' in human drama, that the feeling was big and most real. The sign of a great artist is to establish with the audience or reader immediate and absolute intimacy; all else belongs to second-rate and descriptive art, concerned with media, techniques, performances. Chaplin was in my skin; he was as intimate and as general, as Tolstoy, Gorki at his best, Balzac, Michelangelo, Shakespeare; the eye, the viewpoint, is humanity's ordinary one, genius being the ruthless digestion and expression of the eye's information. It's the fact that the eye is common that makes the genius acknowledged, functional, effective.

It was in Clapham at about this time that I saw my first library; I remember an impression of something long and vivacious and brightly lit, I caught a dim din of the books in conversation which caught my imagination at once, and looking back at the light-filled entrance as we left I determined to read from then on as much as I could. And this I did, purely for pleasure—contributing to my ineducability.

Contact with the family at Kennington was increasing; my sister was more consciously addicted to comfort and cleanliness than I, and she correctly associated my guardian with these things. One night in bed with her—she fourteen, I seven—I 'felt funny', and this 'reduced' me— for so we must speak—to fondness. She reacted in a 'womanlike' way, playing on my feelings, delighting to reduce me, more correctly, to awkwardness, to fumbling infantilism. She was very bright, brittle, beautiful, passionately made, and cold as the clicking of a shop till and dreamily sentimental. She was to go to my school. She said she was younger than she was, due to a deficiency in her education, which appalled me—other people's sins always shocked me. Then, she became very popular very quickly, had great 'personality' able to sell for flattering criticisms attributes she had and hadn't. I was obsessed with her phony-ness and duplicity. An excellent and charming liar, she acquired a reputation for honesty, and quickly learned to moralise. But whereas she gained lighter affections from more people, I gained a great deal from one or two; her diffusion thinned her. She had become as English as she could be, disliking everything foreign on a snobbish principle, though as she grew older a certain conflict arose between her snobbish disaffection from and her sexual attraction for foreigners. Once she 'gave way' to love, she became happy and began practically, to be in a 'bad way'. Our relationship developed equally in hatred and sexual attraction; her moralising became a nightmare to me. She was frightened of me because she thought me wild, and I of her because she represented the cruelty of law and order, the cruelty of surface decency and money-making.

There seems to be a complex of inter-relations beyond chronology between my next few crimes, my guardian's growing demonstrativeness with me and, from that, extension of the sodality between men of which I'd had two experiences already. The crime cut brilliantly through to my freedom; the sodality drew me into a narcotic claustrophobia enervatingly delicious and hallucinatory of reality.

But this harmony with my guardian seemed to involve

me in disharmony with other people; Mrs. Law, for instance, thought our association strange. My guardian as, I've said, treated me as much like an adult as one could treat a child, and the conventional treatment of children from others seemed humiliating, and not altogether understandable, particularly sweet treatment. I made no contact with anyone but my guardian, and developed mild wickedness with others. For instance I began stealing pennies methodically from Mrs. Law; and began playing with her little girl in a way she considered to be immoral, and which I found very delightful.

Roaming about the streets of Clapham—long, rather choppy-housed streets, streets of organised slight vagary —a little more interesting than some boroughs, such as Wimbledon—introduced me to my later practice of ambling-thinking-feeling, which began adventurously with an imagined destination but developed, of course, into 'pure travelling'. I think one has to move to be solitary. But the London 'feel' was beginning to soak in, of endless stone-canals, blue, dirty, paper-bagged, endless traffic or, if silent, endless outer desolation and cramped vivacity within. Clapham had its 'common', a dirty affair on its outskirts where we—the 'gang' and I —would stone another gang. I became very excited in this continuous war, and promised my gang fourteen armed horses and suits of armour from my guardian. I also took to making mysterious references to an exalted identity behind the intentionally modest one they knew. I saw at length that I was the Prince of Wales incognito, and might at any moment be called back to the Palace. I was not, I think, believed; but found nothing impressive in their scepticism; I disliked the so servile exaltation of his highness as to put him out of my world—a nice twist.

94

At school, I had frequently been upset by so many children with faces of plain virtue dancing forward in a rectitudinal choreography of angelicism with flowers and sweets for—not usually the nicest teacher but the hatchet-faced one who fancied herself most. This we could see she did by the way she would twist her neck to dash her actually unpleasant face into poses she thought fetching; she had a rat-like expression behind her smile, warning us we'd better be deceived about her. I put up a good show in this, but it occurred to me she'd better be fed too, for she was a remarkably hungry woman. I therefor stole my biggest sum to date—a half-crown—and bought her a silly sugar robin in a white sugar cage, and placed it succinctly before her, preening. Walking home with her that night I transformed my guardian's routine military medals into a V.C., and she angled her crane-head glittering in his direction of acquaintance, which displeased me. The discovery of this theft served as a climax in our failure to live in 'civilised' surroundings. In these and other crimes my guardian was remarkably reasonable. I don't think he mentioned prison; he implied that other people, through some sort of myopia, would always be unpleasantly upset at things being stolen from them. True, he adulterated this with obscure mutterings about its being wicked, but this I gathered was for show. He was romantic about criminals. I thought him the most sensible man on earth; and have met, undoubtedly many stupider, with nastier natures. At this juncture, it was decided we would retire, together, from the crowd to live again in our little hut.

CHAPTER SIX

There had been a mild class-friction between my sister and me; she said that my accent was become dreadfully common. I was aware of only two classes, mine and that of the tough boys on the common; I didn't particularly like mine, and I didn't know theirs. Madam Tillieux' was the class I'd liked.

But my sister's remark planted a seed or at least marked a dawning awareness of class. Certainly now my visits home were embarrassing in a way I couldn't determine, but which resulted in emotional flares in defence of my guardian who was, they implied, 'common'. The embarrassment lay in the different speech and behaviour of Mother, and even of 'Jacko' (one reason for his attachment to her was her past social position). Home behaviour seemed a web of dangerous elements, and I started a ruthless research of my guardian.

But oddly enough what else than snobbish could my 'aesthetic' criticism of his less pleasant habits be called? Habits such as his noisy eating, certain vile vowels of his, especially 'ou', and 'no', which went for a toboggan ride in his throat. This criticism was later to constitute my 'filthy attitude'. But at this point in my story, of our return to the hill, class was just beginning to appear on the horizon of consciousness. My guardian, as soon as it did, took the part of the plain man—rather handicapped in his handsome loyalty by the plain man's permanent residence on a fence. Thus in the face of Ignorance he leaned heavily to his public school past, but in the face of manners whose refinement embarrassed him—usually on account of their recent satisfaction—he leaned to the working-class directness, which his army experience had also shown him to be somewhat more advanced, in many ways. His heart was certainly warm to working-class people, being of the same quality as theirs, with a small peppering of neuroses. But though his heart was, more or less, working-class, he was violently snobbish with regard to his immediate social inferiors—the lower clerical workers, shopkeepers especially, landladies and the like. I sympathised with him there; such routines didn't seem to bring the best out of humanity.

The hut on the hill was in a fairly detached part of a holiday camp, the most 'select' of several on this hill in Surrey. The signs of this selectiveness were the wide spaces between huts; their decorum in colour and lack of fantasy in architecture, and the absence of radios (though the loudspeaker was still young), and the quality and size of the cars arriving at week-ends; and the good quality plus-fours of the younger set. They were, in fact, of the class most disliked by my guardian, mostly prosperous shopkeepers, with a sprinkling of teachers, whom he also didn't like. It fairly pleased him not to like anyone in the camp except a certain scoutmaster. This was the quint-essence of scoutmasters, and I feel certain he came from Roehampton, because of a particular greenhouse wildness in his appearance (I caught him acquiring a tropical tan artfully behind a bush once). He liked to stand most erect on the brow of the plateau and scan the horizon, eyes narrowed, ready, I believe, for eventualities. He addres-sed every man as Old Man, like Mr. Polly but more refinedly; his accent fascinated me; a glass lady on a tightrope between Upper Wimbledon and Clapham, Clapham being a dark thread erupting to the surface in moments of dangerous fluency. He was an elderly young man, and later became a youngish middle-ager; as he cast aside his class so did he his age. He waved both away with his esoteric pocket handkerchief. Greater meaning lay on either side of the vulgar truth, always so that Madame Blavatsky and other suburban mystics were on his list. When he spoke he threw away an ironical expression on his face, just slowly enough to let you see it; his drawling eyes seemed to be shaken as well. His voice leaned on your shoulder; and really, one year he disappeared for showing too much love to one of his scouts. I can't say that prejudiced me against him, but I remember it as another of the many instances I'd come across of homosexuality playing the part of a social glue between fringe-types on different classes.

A later addition to the hill were the Dewberries, an ageing—always ageing—schoolmaster and his wife, though eventually his wife collapsed to a place chronologically much further ahead than he; she wore brilliant kimonos, a whipped-cream drawl, eyes painted with exotic ennui, and had for intimates two monkeys who stank the hut out; 'Duckayee' she called them, and 'Biaybee' and 'Duhhling'; and they'd squeak and defaecate, and she was far too transcendent to notice this, or the smell. She liked me, sniffing an indrawn soul there, 'an interesting, dreamy little lad'; she didn't know, I had plotted in the hot nights, though I never actually achieved, the removal of her plain but volatile little daughter's drawers. The Dewberries were appalling to my guardian; he'd hop at the double past their hut, looking terribly uncomfortable if they addressed him. The husband he pitied; the wife he considered a frightening freak.

But in our early times there were very few people who used the place. We could walk, also, straight to the then old-world Barley Mow, a place where fine beer came straight out of barrels, and my guardian loved to take a pint or two of what then was called 'four x'. Or we could walk straight down the hill to another very nice pub, and sleep it off—my guardian sleep it off—in the wheat field. Here our relationship was simple and excellent—it hadn't yet reached the sticky stage. Or we'd wander out with a Lyons's Dundee Cake tin (a new one every Saturday) full of sandwiches, for several miles away, looking for flowers and birds. But a conflict grew up between us because of my passion for other children. I slowly assembled a gang on the hill and, being the only resident, was captain: due also to my inability to do anything but command. I'd spend all day out with my gang, who would spy on people who wanted privacy, as in defaecating, urinating, lovemaking or sleeping, throw stones at windows, make hideous noises, torture little children who wouldn't join us, and generally be as powerful a nuisance as we could. Then, when I returned to the hut, my guardian would be sulking. He would say astringently: 'I suppose you've been enjoying yourself, eh?' The accusation was my ability to enjoy myself away from him. I'd then have to coax him back to affection. But I couldn't give up my gang, and spent anxious times co-ordinating both lives. The strain of placating him meant squeezing my diaphragm in, to squeeze my heart upward, which became the standard method of engineering all exhausting affection (peak of which was when my guardian's pious sister gave me a prayer-book when she'd promised a Christmas present; the device was a masterpiece; the tears welled into my eyes which had the double function of relieving my misery and impressing her with the intensity of my gratitude). But therefore, wild times with my gang grew into conceptions of wild freedom from him; and the correspondingly greater intimacy with him meant non-existence through consciousness of sin.

My best friend was a dirty-souled lad of twelve, with glasses, who tickled his sister between her legs and lifted up his rather artistic mother's skirts who would allow it in the name of the then dawning emancipation—or rather of an older emancipation dripping, rather soiled, down to the lower-middle classes. Like many tasteless people, they seized upon anarchic 'breadth' as the first stage in cultural development. Their dirtiness fascinated me—grubbiness, I mean, of sex mixed with family emotion; the father, well-headed, grey-white faced, stupid as a cow, alert on top of that, seemed to seep at the pores with hot juices of sexuality; his heat was grey and moist, inherited by his eldest. The youngest child had unusually thick skin, always dry, often with a dry red flush. The five of them stayed in a round tin hut, and formed a kind of family emotional-sexual stew of their own; they eagerly dabbled out of their confines, as they were attempting to do out of their particularly nasal whines, into culture's primrose woods, and they picked on my guardian as a backwoodsman but one who never-theless had been nearer than they to their determined destination; like all self-respecting persons, they belittled every personal stage ahead of them in their track, includ-ing my guardian's. But my guardian didn't like them at all, on account of their emotional dirtiness, I imagine.

I liked that quality because in its warmth and wantonness, at least, it reminded me of Mother.

One day, evidently in greater heat than usual, rising in fact to the cultural level, the father decided to beard, culturally, my guardian in his castle; to have it intellectually out with him, smarting, as he was, under my guardian's unintentional superiority in behaviour.

Thus I caught him addressing my guardian from the path below our hut, my guardian on the veranda (an addition we'd both made to the hut recently), something after this fashion: 'Aristotle, when he wrote the "Frogs"', said clearly that Aeschylus was the best dramatist of his time.' My guardian went pink. 'No,' he said, extraordinarily fussed and grim, 'Aristotle did not write the "Frogs". The "Frogs" was written by Aristophanes.' 'I beg your pardon,' said Brewery, affecting to be genuinely troubled at my guardian's darkness, its taking him painfully so by surprise, 'but I fear Aristotle did write the "Frogs". Damn it, I've been reading it this week-end.' 'I think you'll find,' said my guardian quite agitated, 'that he did not. However . . .' he turned to go in. 'Well, I'll look that up,' said Mr. Brewery. But Mr. Brewery had been sharp; in this battle for precedence he'd provoked my guardian to demonstrate, through his agitation, the recent, almost unnatural acquisition of 'culture'; he concluded no doubt that my guardian's was not 'vintage'; whereupon he lost much of his nervousness, the exposure of his own mistake being by comparison small and rectifiable. In the hut my guardian called him 'Ignorant'. And now this agitation became mine for years because I too, though rather differently, had made my little hoard of knowledge out of the golden current of its class-acquisition; and my voice trembled too when I stood my ground, feeling the quicksand so often.

Nineteen twenty-seven was in the years of the emergence of the Little Man; we had the phrases, 'in my opinion', 'speaking as a plain man'—'plain' meant profound in an inscrutably British way; a period of the final imbecility of the senile trend of patriotism, of, indeed, the spade as spade. The vanity of the 'little men' was being tickled by the vulgar press and the vulgar politicians, and an orgy of vulgarity in Italy and Germany being rehearsed encouraged the British kind; the period is an object lesson in the practical identity of anarchism and facism, and of the awful by-consequences of further soul-peddling from the handmaiden poets and littérateurs. It should be noted that the 'plain man' is as coy as a spinster, and likes to live, maybe not in the same street but certainly in the same town as the not-plain man: each being the mirror-image of the other. You won't get your cake-hearted poet without your indigestible dough-hearted plain man.

In my guardian the emergence of the plain man was exemplified by sequences of pink-flushing, dyspepsia, awkward shiftings of the shoulders and tight gathering in of the jacket by the lapels (drawing his plain man's cloak closer to him in the prevailing winds of Decadence), and wearing (in the experimental stage) that expression which has developed into the commonplace street-face of today: the expression of 'the truth I tell is nothing to do with me, little man that I am, but compelled by my good heart'. His eyes would seek the floor, and he would look more remarkably stupid than I had previously seen; particularly in the fatness of his yellowish cheek.

Today, incidentally, that cliché expression has become

a straightforward truth-driven one by the lower-middle classes, which I'd say heralded a major political change (there's an outboard motor to the craft), sinister since it consorts perfectly with an expression of nearly triumphant cunning; it's the average, voting and living expression of today. The cunning element is that none believes in the truth that drives him; he merely sits in a Victoria pre-fab vehicle of ideology for the journey).

My guardian shuffled up to eminence first in his own eyes and then in those of a small circle round him; grimacing all the way, patting his cheeks, declaring how handsome he was after shaving (and truly an uglier man would be difficult to meet); and he, a flabby man in all but the easy rigidity or morality, would enthuse at the mention of Mussolini and Hitler, particularly Hitler, admiring his force, drive, etc.—the shopkeeper's ideal. As an example of the real sewer-soul, the tart-heart, the mashbrain, the scummy-eyed hypocrite, nothing can rival the eminent plain man. And his birth is one of life's embarrassing moments.

(It is an interesting association that makes a man look his dullest when he thinks he's telling the truth; he points to his conception of truth's being completely abstract; so that he undresses his face and himself of all mundane furniture; but telling the truth in this way, one could remarkably well be run over by a bus, as truth's revengeful body come to claim its suspended soul.)

It was around this year that my guardian considered Madame Blavatsky, spiritualism, psychoanalysis, fascism, communism and philately; the last two were to endure. He would accuse me now of cunning; I would unfortunately accuse him of unconscious cunning—more infuriating than my own.

My guardian's admiration for great 'little men' was understandable of course; he was somewhat rancid with failed idealism himself. As a nice little simpleton himself believing his elders' braying, he'd volunteered under-age in 1914—I think he was sixteen—had, in 1918 been shot in the leg and stomach, crawled for twenty-four hours before he was found, dragging the semi-detached leg with him. The war had broken his conventional 'ideals' (I believe Rupert Brooke's verse partly responsible); all this, and health gone into the bargain, for absolutely nothing. My guardian's avoidance of women was become chronic now that we were alone in our hut. Should one by an unusual mishap approach our door we would instantly stop talking; sometimes I would look through the keyhole and advise my general on the enemy's disposition, slanderously too. With baited breath we'd hope she'd go away. If she didn't, my guardian would fetch down from some dim past cupboard his broadest and silliest grin, and walk down our steps (to discourage her from walking up them) expressing his uncontrollable pleasure at seeing her; he was weakened, however, by her acceptance of these graces as sterling. Should she gain entry, which disturbed me more than him I think, he would sidle his faces through tea at an elevation of ascetic refinement horrible to hear; nothing was too banal for him to say. With a positive leer into his teacup or at me he would declare the weather to be *lovely*, caddishly to encourage her to expand in the same motif. Then, 'Gone,' he'd say, 'thank God for that!' And we'd stretch our shoulders, inhale deeply, and set about again to man's living. On the same principle we kept the curtains his sister was constantly presenting him at bay. When the day came that further disdain was impossible, we felt true defeat in cluttering our plain windows, that went with our plain sausages, plain steaks, plain 'bully-beef' with such feminine frills. Cushions we never countenanced.

We had returned to the hill in my holidays; at the close of these it became unhappily necessary for me to go to school again, and my guardian chose the 'High School' at the bottom of the hill; as I was to discover, a typical ecclesiastical laundry of rexine culture for the soaping out of human juices.

'Hillway High School' educated the sons of prosperous shopkeepers, farmers, and of a few middle-class people. It modelled itself on the public schools, had a school motto which became the red rag to my small bull —*Ora et Labora*, both of which I avoided like the plague, an O.T.C. (which degenerated to a Cadet Corps and thence to a Boy Scouts troop—I gave up at the third stage), a school song, houses and housemasters: some of these felicities are now descended to our Secondary Modern Schools. The head had the air and manner of a man-sized duckling, still downy and transcendentally clean, with fine hairs in his nose, his ears and his head; he was far too funny to be true, and like many funny men, terrifying at close quarters. He was excessively mentally hygienic, challenging with a wag of his high-pitched, oversize aquiline nose all the base tendencies he rightly assumed to be present in children. He liked cleanly to ask in the scripture lesson: 'Brown, what is the meaning of Fornication?'—making Brown the victim of his entirely subjective appreciation of the matter. He thrilled in the spiritualistic probing of all matters he deemed unclean; my nose would feel clogged when he passed by. His was an entirely relative purity, a lean-to on indispensable corruption; indeed, he was a spiritual wage-slave of ordure. He was my first proper introduction to British sanitary decadence, the soaped and disinfected decadence of a frightened people. Always stewing in sensations, I rejoiced at this time in my physical happiness, until he hooked me out into the drying air of English psalmody. It had a terrible and long drawn out effect on me, because it dovetailed with my family predisposition to spiritualise, a predisposition which hitherto hadn't become manifest in me. As Catholic I could have maintained a feasible compromise, reporting to the church the antics of the passions. But the ethics of anglicanism taken with Catholic logic produce the most frightful results—'spiritualisation' to the point of madness. Catholic converts to anglicanism are very rare, which cannot be said of the converse.

Our headmaster was enamoured of his head, associating it (not to deny the correctness of it) with brains; he had strained it as far from its base moorings as was humanly possible, leaving his neck long and scraggy, with an Adam's apple for a holy office, to intercept passional reactions coming up. But of course, as with such types generally, a most humid gloss of curiously rare, vaporous sexuality lay about him—a sort of astringent lubricant like Bay Rum—he was so nimble, so fetchingly darting, so quick and ceaseless, with the cold rendering of a stoat's heat. In fact I suspected him (I was precocious in thinking what people called 'the worst' of people) of 'improper' antics with his wife; she looked extremely tired and dishevelled, and always agreed most depressedly to what he said—which was volumes. But alas, she loved him; I swore to myself that the crook had arranged it. But her mien may just have been the projected hash of his righteousness, which could obviously find no oblivion in bed.

I abominated him, thoroughly, carefully, listing the physical peculiarities with immense precision, the way my guardian assessed the details of his stamps. But I saw little of him in my first year; he gave me excellent reports, saying I was an intelligent, painstaking little boy. Time made him revise his opinions formidably. At first I was in the stimulating freshness of clarity induced by fear and strangeness; fear unfortunately has a productive effect on me, taken in small doses before paralysis. I showed off with graceful diffidence, like an American film-star in 'In Town Tonight'; 'not I, but the inextinguishable light within me,' I seemed to say—a pedagogic implication. Before, I'd loved history, as given me by a fat little history of the world with pictures. I read all this many times, thrilling to it more on account of what I took to be its veracity than to stories inartistically poisoned with make-believe. This lasted me for the first year at school, as did my other already considerable reading. But the time came when what I found out with pleasure for myself, clashed with some kind of deodorant called the curriculum and my little beliefs cowed and went back inside me, and from then on developed a private pregnancy independent of scholastic nourishment. I came to disbelieve what I was told, became decreasingly interested in it and eventually evolved an efficient means of rejection at ear level.

I began to notice physical reactions which later, I'm convinced, sprang from erotic roots, to mathematics; some days (as today) I could solve problems with a musical facility; at other days a sort of lift arrangement would travel between my genitals, or 'stomach' and my head,

leaving there a thick steamy feeling; in maths, I seemed
to want to do, on off days, something physical, and felt
the strain of abstracting an agony. I later realised that
elementary maths involves thought processes so simple
as to baffle one who, like myself, delighted in meandering
along complex paths; already some mental process was
forming to become typical later, in which allowed pockets
of 'feelies' of thoughts littered the field, while clean
armed knights of major propositions were often allowed
reckless liberty of deployment; then, in their rest period,
one or two pockets would be opened up to release modi-
fying vapours; parallel with this was a system of allowing
so much at the back of the mind while allowing the
'front' to rush ahead; it is the combination of imagined
body-sensations in the thinking that interests me; I
rarely think without some little significant, often modify-
ing 'ping' of sensation to 'sound' somewhere else on the
board, which may be, possibly, little memory-fields of
early association—memories of experiences localised in
different parts of the body.

I took great pleasure in writing 'English', and at once,
as opposed to mathematics, relished something dirty
about it—something anti-hygienic into which something
definitely sexual could be employed (later, disastrously).
I wrote with my whole 'body'.

My first English teacher I loved but had to betray,
because she was devoutly religious. She encouraged my
writing but tried to make a Christian of me, through
Wordsworth largely. She had a 'fire'; her aged virginity
was not muddied at all I think. She was a very good
woman, addled I suppose by the circumstantial limitations,
but good; I hung on to her goodness; as a delinquent in
the making, I was an amateur of virtue, worshipping

anyone who had it. I tried to forgive her ringing declamation of 'Drake's Drum'; for I could never swallow
her mind, which was henlike and eccentric in the orthodox manner of anglican spirituality. She was full of
virtue's strange jerks, movements of the epileptic dis-
missal of all 'passional' elements in whatever she sensed.
She was wordsworthian; her 'trailing clouds of glory'
made a deep impression, which lasts. I betrayed her one
day when I was in her study—I had ceased attending
scripture lessons when Mother began insisting I prepare
for my confirmation in the R.C. church, which ably
prepared me for atheism through a minimum of religious
instruction. In her study I one day threw ink over her
time-table; she addressed me with burning cheeks and
flashing blue eyes—and I loved her eyes—before the class
as one unworthy of her trust. The grubbiness with
which she thus dressed me lasted almost forever; I
became cleverer, but had lost my innocence. I began then
questioning everything she said; she answered me with
an uneasy 'intellectual' vibrancy, which I disliked. My
masterpiece of the period in essays was a reconstruction
of the blind girl wandering through the catacombs from
Lytton's 'Pompei', which I composed in tears. I have
always loved women most when they were sad; I may for
loving purposes even have encouraged them into that
state. Women seem wise when sad and silly when happy
—or brilliant.

I felt on more intimate terms with the teachers than
with my fellow pupils, who appeared incredibly moronic
to me—I mean in their general behaviour, not of course,
in their work. I could not understand them in the least—
their nearly self-conscious childishness, as though enjoying a lease of authoritatively approved imbecility, of

daring so curiously limited, disobedience so patently craven, and utter respectability. But the degree of desperation that the few rebels found necessary to work up for their escapades terrified me. I was quite double myself; my fear of the authorities was so excessive that I took not the slightest real notice of my behaviour in their presence; it was, it seemed, so absolutely dictated by them as to be their handiwork and irrelevant to my life, like paying taxes. With the boys I was fluent beyond the usual daring, in denouncing the authorities and charmingly obedient in front of them. Then, and now, like all private rebels, I have realised no need to serve up my rebellion with a reasoned proclamation of differences which would, I imagine, merely warn the enemy in time; they had, and have, none of my conscience. But I can't agree with this attitude; it gives me liberty, but a rather sterile one. But one for whom I from then on felt a great affection fought a master and left the classroom, fiery faced and glittering eyed; and the master, noted for his coldness (which I liked—I imagined him too intelligent for his job) went pale, and was defeated, and left soon after.

Like the rest of the fatherless or more so (with my guardian in the background) I searched easily for an understanding with men never given: to last till my so-called maturity. I crept in tones and feeling as near as I dare to them for an explanation, an enlightenment which didn't come: climax of this was, later, when on a sunny day I tinkled the wooden end of a brush in a glass of water, in our dusty, bust-littered 'art room'; the sound was delicious, and I asked the art-master if that wasn't so. He said I'd gone mad. Then I climbed down from the hopeless quest for a while. It was mad to announce the music of wood on glass in water on a hot day; sane to be insensitive.

The proletarian was the woodwork master; one day when I did something—planing, perhaps—with the inspired and unskilful *brio* my background had qualified, he looked at me out of his rather dull eyes like a god of the earth. I knew that sin, then—of mistaking excitement for skill, of which it's the artful evader. He impatiently took the tool from me; his heavy hands and arms worked to music; he sweetly did the job so rightly, like a priest in his labour of devotion both to wood and to article. That was a deeper humiliation for me than that of my glad gaffs in class. Culture was done in a cryptic *brio*; spread like butter on stones, or tombstones on child corpses.

Why did we learn? I never knew; my guardian never told me, not the masters, not the boys. No one knew; I was a frantic reader but not to learn as I understood that word—but to live elsewhere, other lives in other places. At about eleven I read Dickens, everything he wrote of fiction; his was my favoured world, and his humour convulsed me and his pathos made me weep. To me, too, the characteristic performances of people were inexplicable; hyperbolically eccentric. I had a cold eye for the grandeurs of my elders; I didn't know they were invalids.

Meanwhile we were pelted with little pieces of Wordsworthian esotericism, bits of God the Arch-Chain-Store Grocer, of algebra, of the world being enormous and Niagara stupendous, rattling among Henry's crown and Gladstone's speech. But let me cease with the strong implication that I was a bad pupil because I was intelligent; there were other, perhaps greater contributions to the result. But the non-inquirers did well; that's impossible to doubt. Now, when the Gods are tired, inquirers are pretty fashionable, provided they inquire in blinkers; it wouldn't be well, then, to cash in on the bad form of a good thing.

I believe I have said of myself at an earlier stage, 'This was the beginning of self-consciousness', by which I meant the dawn of the sense of isolated action: the first tight-rope walk. Now the next kind of self-consciousness assailed me, of myself as being, with my guardian, 'different', of having with him a peculiar language, of having to use with others a public as opposed to this private speech. There follows a long dull period, begun excitedly, exploratorily, of eccentrification. There is a turning point in the history of an eccentric; the first time when what he is doing or saying seriously, is greeted with laughter; laughter which indicates his failure to communicate his meaning; he will thenceforward speak and act increasingly oddly and humorously.

This laughter happened to me at a point when I forgot to translate my private self into the public expression and was thus discovered; the gulf between my guardian and myself and the world thus widened, and as my courage ran out at school I began playing for laughter, to disarm; but I was laughed at, at the same time, without my connivance. Yet at first I was taken seriously, and almost reached the hero-stage; I fought well, always winning till one day I lost, and became a pacifist, never fighting again. Losing had terrified me; I didn't know what the victor mightn't take. Similarly in games I ostentatiously stopped trying as soon as I began to fall behind the others. I would not attempt what I felt I couldn't do; and what I couldn't do was what I was incapable of enthusiasm for. I held in horror, at an early age, Christian virtues—those of altruism. I could be generous affectionately; but would never be so on principle. To do good on principle was to enter into hopeless rivalry with the powerful organisations of society; and actually looked like a game of pretty make-believe for rewards.

'Unwillingly to school' . . . is a tragedy. The bricks by a wall lost the lyrical drama of their cohesive achievement; little bits of matter appeared forlornly isolated; sentences stuck out of mouths like cold marble; expressions were splintered from continuity, gestures were jerked into their parts like a bad film; the emotional flow became staccato.

The exercise book cover had the air of a frozen pond; their blue lines were threads of confined skies; one looked, and couldn't focus, one's gaze went on for ever. The desks, in their runnels, were heaped with solid time, little points into which undigested time had stuck; when the door opened the whole room seemed to expand its chest, and wither at its close. Schoolmasters' flesh looked like old pastry. You could study it till you felt as sleepy as it; their eyes dim in your study of them were relieved of life, and you saw bits of blue water, and old strings on their head, and their foreheads like silly boxes, and their jaws like shop-tills opening and shutting with a chink of money, and their words as unmental as their emissions of anal gas. The whole of them was a wheezy, pedestrianly assembled thing called man that worked ill, perfunctorily, having nothing to do with what it said but the dull tones it used; it was steam escaping, taps dripping, it gave madness through monotony and the crown of its dullness was its power. Only the hypocrites and the mentally deficient took it seriously; it appreciated mediocrity, spoke to it man to man, called it a good chap and wished it well. It eyed the rest as policemen play cat and mouse with burglars.

The wheeze of lower-middle-class aspiration escaped with the gas.

It was my aim, risking the errors and simplifications, to ascribe my ailments to, or explain them in terms of a social system; and to win, if only a mite, from the contemporary falsification of ascribing them to family-originating 'neuroses', the contemporary begging of the question: a great aim conceived in a paucity of knowledge.

I had all the drives to religion—the 'temperament'—without the 'faith'; so the waves of these urges to an inner peace, solution, compensation, opiate, broke into consciousness. At a very early age actions ceased to find their consummation; divided aims, self-consciousness, made the mental hangover on which religion grows. As my apparent self became actually leaner in expressions, more retired, more pacifist, my soul became as fat as a pig with no really satisfying body of delusion to discharge itself into.

My actional expressions became increasingly erratic, over-charged with meaning; I began living a myth of a greater self, as children do, but more seriously, and for much longer. I found an ease, the ease of dreaming, in commanding my little gang on the hill, in ordering punishments. I watched myself disembodiedly doing what others told me, for unaccountable reasons, with pity for me, as for a stranger, a pit-pony: evaded as much as possible the heavy labours of interpreting souls as the compensation for social failures and bondages. Instead I imitated—in the day when all the 'little men' of the suburbs and offices were dreaming the existence of the 'great men', the dictators—the success I felt I should have had; in becoming delusorily great I attacked and hid from the persecutor of this ideal great figure, my true self. I giggled at night after the day's sorties. I felt imminence in the day; slightly at first, but reaching dangerous proportions in my early manhood. The hill played its directly physiological as well as its obviously psychological part in this. For I remember vividly how, after climbing the hill from school (as I did every day) I felt faint, breathless and observant when I reached the top; how the mere whiff of wind was sensuously delicious, how the merest crackle of a twig in the woods I went through set my nerves bounding like violin strings. My progress became ominous to me—I seemed to hold so much more than anyone was likely to see: a vast pantechnicon of sensory reactions, of subtle selves, one speaking to another endlessly.

I went down with a rush to school; then, my cheeks reddened, blood pounded in my head, and stupidity swept over me. After the heat I felt curiously shaggy and dirty. And after the heat the road was flat, filled with senseless minutiae and miniaturely-acting people, so painfully irritating to a silence I carried with me: so intense in their interests, which were cruelly departmentalised, madly exact, rigidly furnished, and oblivious of mine.

CHAPTER SEVEN

My guardian was a bad giver. When Mother gave, the objects just moved from her side of life to mine for my use. But my guardian insisted upon gratitude, which I gave in a variety of painful grimaces and a feeling of exhaustion in the chest. He taught me to expect things for good behaviour, which spoiled the things, of course. They were taken in too much of a hurry, and the attitude encouraged me to exploit him, and consequently became a routine hostility such as unites many families. At first, of course, I didn't understand him—understand why I should be grateful; he had clearly to say that if it weren't for him I'd be in awful places and states. That too was no explanation: why had he troubled to save me? I didn't get as far as saying or realising I'd been a help-less object moved from one person to the other; that was my assumption, however, because it was the truth. It made my fondness for him become affected; I rebounded from him emotionally because my affection was enforced and this estrangement created a feeling of guilt which I misinterpreted as love for him.

Giving may indeed be a (small and coarse) sign of affection; but the affection revealed thereby will only be returned if that expression of it does not assume an independent virtue. One has a natural right to everything that exists: one's share, in gifts or in earnings, is abso-lutely arbitrarily determined by economic conditions.

And so I was an ungrateful child; steadily earning the cheap sins of incomprehension. I saw in others how easy it was to be a grateful child, and a good child altogether; the spectacle encouraged me in my rude ways. I had no doubt of either the hypocrisy or the invalidity of the good child, its sincerity or its diplomacy. I noted children strung up to a nervous pitch of virtue: they tend to become successful in later life, artfully stepping down the virtue and stepping up the career, the latter being the former's world-wounded grimace; the nervous tension of it was raw fuel to their endeavour. These would be of the upper-lower-middle class. The hypocrites would be more contented 'ideologically', in their private fashioning, and be less strenuous to please the social gods. The recalcitrants had no public hopes; theirs was the kingdom of heaven, whose mortal subjects are apt to be very wicked people in an economically ineffectual manner.

All this goes to describe my slow and steady fashioning into a worker in values as opposed to a worker in goods; the eternal quibbler, as they say, who wouldn't move a step till he understood all about it to his own satisfaction; who in his eventual madness began criticising the road and its direction, who plunged into dark footpaths and only called for help when his deep self had made sure the highwaymen wouldn't hear him.

I was known concurrently as The Poet and Philip Augustus at school, in mockery of my dreaminess (strictly about school matters) and my, I suppose, aloof manner, or my distaste for 'mixing'. Philip Augustus meant nothing to me, but the advantages of The Poet in sentimentally literary England, with its wealth of convention about the ineffectiveness of poets, their harmlessness and higher idiocy I naturally seized on. I readily subscribed to the idea that it was in the name of a higher calling that I became steadily more obtuse in the ordinary one. It was a passport to freedom from many silly but useful applications, and it continued through various snobberies to lead me with *élan* and efficiency to pauperism and whimsey, where I now bask; the whimsey must be shaved before the pauperism goes.

At eleven, in my Wordsworth period, I took self-conscious nature-worshipping walks through the woods alone. I cultivated very early the look askance (a better interpretation than that of hideous shyness) and the rapt deafness. Masturbation ably sustained this stance, contributing the essential characteristic of absentmindedness; this first happened up an oak tree, and became among other things a banner of independence from my guardian; but I suppose the 'sweet' atmosphere he exuded, encouraged it, as did his anti-sociality which I shared and his terror of women, and my own fear of them. I was astonished at the different consciousness the practice induced; that of a queer abstraction, of flights of intensely rapid and accurate thinking followed by wooden dullness; of a too heady isolation from people, an inoculation against all emotional appeals; but how much can be ascribed to a practice so largely symptomatic is at the moment impossible to determine. Society guides sex into its channels, and even professions.

Nevertheless from that period my oscillations in personality became marked, from the jaded, cynical, clever, to the extreme opposite—sentimental, sensuous, naïve to an appalling degree. My guilt about masturbation was dramatically so furious that to relieve it I did it more. For I would not, about that as little as about anything else, be guilty; and does not the road of excess lead to the desolate shack of wisdom? It became an adventure to wake up and wonder which self I'd be; in operation I criticised one in terms of the other, so that neither ever pleased soberly but each achieved their intoxicated apotheoses. Such drunkenness! Such marvellousness of mere 'being', as the hack mystics say. Later it had to be alcohol. Anything was adventure: the creeping, darting and paralytic stopping in woods, among dark trees—racing over fields like the wind chased by the devils: mooning somnolently and grandly by our old static-water pond, with its blasted trees sticking up in the middle; a 'hoah', and off like a rabbit out of all grasping human ken, which one could never stay out of, alas. Greatness, I felt, constantly, immense greatness, immense intelligence till I felt my head would burst like an exploding pumpkin. I ached to show that I knew better, as though I were in an agony to urinate. The word 'fool' fashioned itself sharply, hissingly on my tongue. I applied it as much to objects that wouldn't do what I wanted as to people similarly afflicted.

The need to show off—or perhaps it could more kindly be called the need to communicate intense feelings and thoughts, which all children and their artistic descendants endure—became so chronic that I confused the compulsion with an actor's vocation, and heart and soul organised amateur dramatics, with myself in the lead, producing and inventing the story as we went along; I chose almost invariably a villainous role. The whole camp attended our shows; the climax of communication was incommunication: my last and greatest role was writhing and rolling on the stage in imitation of epilepsy. The audience did not understand my message, and neither did I. It was perhaps a portrayal of excessive irritation at their presence or more truly an agony of wanting something very badly and not knowing what it was.

My guardian's hands were become very touching, his demonstrations of affection commoner, with flushes of emotion accompanying them; out of this too I could have wanted to writhe. His dependence weighed heavily upon me: the child was so big. If my activities with my gang kept me away from him all day, he would be moody and jealous on my return, encouraging guilt and determination to continue. But I was as jealous as he if he saw anyone else. He ascribed more guile to me than I had: I can calculate quickly on the spot, but in a way more for the fun than the use of it. He would give and forgive me things in moments of affection which he would fear I had obtained by guile in his moments of repentance. He was deeply involved in his emotional life, and in its undercurrent, the sexual life he lacked; he went from philately to spiritualism.

Around twelve I began to suffer from nightmares, from which I woke sweating, and mostly about my 'gorilla' who persisted in shuffling the dark shrubbery in front of him, extending one big hand like a man's, yet never letting me see his face. The mornings were the happiest times, then. My guardian, from his army stretcher on the floor, had on his left everything within reach for breakfast without having to get up. After breakfast his round face would beam. 'Here's luxury,' he'd say, in a cloud of tobacco smoke. Often, in winter, we'd wake 'above the clouds', looking out on a milky misty sea a few feet below us.

Another nightmare, but half-waking, was when the room would appear several miles away but very clear, not unrelated to Swift's obsession with size in *Gulliver's Travels*.

We stayed on the hill until I was fourteen. I went steadily down the class at school, became steadily more elaborate in my eccentricity, ill-at-ease and lonely. The real nightmare became school; its worst feature, chill cleanliness, of the corridors, the floors, and the soapy-smelling masters often with slight colds to justify the flourish of icy-looking handkerchiefs. We'd moved into a new red-brick building, joining with the Girls' High School. We were encouraged to mix unsexually with the girls, given practice in our deportment with them, at parties. Since in my private imaginings they were all thoroughly 'interfered with', my embarrassment at their super-human decency and chastity of behaviour made my ears red and my cheeks burn. They moved with the tinkly bright cleanliness of little bits of glass. I felt rude. I felt the powers of decency already assembling against me: for I had no conscious conception of their private indecency. A monstrous hygiene, malicious in an unas-sailable way, was ranging itself against me; I felt it in the pure voices of the masters, their cleanliness, in the sanctified delightfulness of the girls, in the smooth hypocrisy of a great many of the boys; I sweated to con-formity, but never made the grade; I was fundamentally against it. When I over-conformed I immediately felt faint, uprooted, torn from myself and the potential prey of beasts that would abstract me from myself. I fled then into a prattling and feminine imbecility, a manner as unsuited to the conformists as my natural uncouthness—which actually wasn't uncouth but a rudeness born of an incomprehension of the veneer of their decency, their collective struggle for refinement which resulted in an embarrassing and grotesque aping of it, and of an almost acknowledged division of themselves into private 'naturals' and public saints. The most equivocal signs of their decency were, indeed, those connected with sport. From sport I fled in a cold sweat of embarrassment at their hot sweat of sublimated something or other; their great red hams kicking the ball would almost turn my stomach; the heavy, hearty antics of the masters were impossible to take seriously; and from this it will be seen that I was becoming, in the language of the hygienists, 'a nasty little invert'. Their comic restraint of their evident passions in cricket dismayed me into a paralysis, a literal incapability of moving a limb in the effort to emulate their 'effortless grace' and 'sportsmanship', which seemed to me unaccountably to make losing as great a thing as winning. Why not lose immediately? I could not understand; it was a ballet of manners required evidently, for a higher purpose.

Their English lessons were degenerating into a series of opportunities for the self-portraiture of the English master: in *Lorna Doone* his voice went deep; he squared his shoulders, assumed a look of rugged virility (he was very old, I thought, to have had a very young baby). At heroic verse he tossed his head sideways, wagged it as though to free it from his collar, fixing us with an ingratiating look. And for communications of philosophic import he became clerical, looked down his nose at us. The only time I liked him was when he lost his temper and called us thundering idiots.

As personalities the masters never went far enough; sometimes they intimated possibilities of human expansion, but ended with little quirks of facetiousness; the constraint was everywhere. They appeared to be living in a living-room of manners, between walls made of reverend critics, under a very low roof of intellect. They

dare not move much: they warned us not to. Being a fool
was the only way to get freedom in this dreadful room.
Their freedom consisted in monotonous and eventually
nauseating physical tricks, such as jerking like conductors
their cuffs from their sleeves, pinching up between
sugar-tong fingers their trouser-legs by the crease, in
absurdly stylised intonations of their voices, and most
common, the delayed nose-blowing with the ferreting
look over the handkerchief at the class (perfectly caught
by Emil Jannings in the old 'Blue Angel' film). And
under the Church of England, in the basement, they
were incredibly sex-conscious; they attacked this subject
with very clean looks, with exact articulation of words
such as fornication, lasciviousness, as though thus drain-
ing them of their evil. The whole parade, in short,
advertised concisely the human virtues of dirt, careless-
ness, sexuality, drunkenness, almost of criminality. This
chorus or 'parade' was not unlike the dancing girls in a
film of the time, 'The Broadway Melody'—as mincing,
not as fluent. The atmosphere was preparing me for
bohemianism, surrealism and D. H. Lawrence; all
reactions against petty-bourgeois pruriency by petty-
bourgeois exiles. For the finicky logic of it was easily,
sumptuously lost in surrealism. The pruriency glided
easily, even in hygienic boats, to Lawrencian 'sexuality'.
Dirt became spiritual pregnancy by reaction. The root
of the show was not, of course, in the symptoms: simply
in the face that no intelligent, brave and honest social
prospect lay ahead for the teachers to inculcate. After
school the wasteland prognosticated by this euphemistic
education was not surprising; the depth of its craters,
however, was unexpected and terrifying. Grown-ups, to
me, are recognisably the result of these educational

antics; they are made men, formed in a hard enamel scribbled with personal advertisements, like baked beans; and quaking within, no doubt, like myself without.

My private reading and my falling behind in class-work at school were parallel developments; gradually, thinking lost all touch with public expression, and I found it eventually impossible to make the slightest sense of what I was taught, which irritated and bored me until I refused to pretend to assimilate any more. The trouble with school then (as, I think, today) was the vilely abstract nature of education; and this isn't overcome by the make-belief realism of the Squeers method, the so-called 'practical' approach, making things and so on, though this certainly constitutes an improvement. What is lacking, and that makes the whole thing too abstract, is a general theory of education geared to a homogeneous conception of society and its development. Education makes for order, and society is, basically, without true order; it is marshalled, but it isn't an organism; that's to say, there's no organic unity, no integration between what one does, work, and what one gets, culture—and culture fundamentally includes money. Ethics taught at school, as all the world knows, have no application out-side for anyone unwilling to be a passive employee-robot for the rest of his days, so that the connection between spirit, initiative and delinquency is logically a close one.

So my mind became independent of education at an early age; I suffered the latter like a rainstorm on my tent walls, which I obliterated with reading. I would read still with this combination of sensation and thinking I've mentioned; and, of course, wherever possible, live for days and, in the case of the *Cloister and the Hearth*, and of Dickens, for years in the books I read. I built a fortress, I took in stores, and I began arming myself inside for some future day when I'd sally forth equipped, as we did in our gang-play on the hill, and as my guardian did living in the hut before his eventual return to normal society.

My reading at this time—between my eleventh and fourteenth years—was widely varied; Stanley Weyman, the 'historical novelist' and Harrison Ainsworth, whom I loved (probably not read at all nowadays), and Dickens, less of Thackeray, some Trollope, Romain Rolland, Ludwig Renn, Remarque, Thomas Mann (whom I grew slowly to appreciate for his magnificent thinking allied to his complete mastery of significant developments), Goethe, Tolstoy, Balzac, Gorki, Ibsen, were authors I respected and loved; I hadn't then, and haven't since, had any feeling for the middle-class of writers—Walpole, Bennett, etc., disliking any book, indeed, in which the alleged interest of the story dealt in any way arbitrarily with character; character revealing philosophy, was what I looked for in reading; I demanded in the summing up a world-view. A book had to be real in the sense of being a proper development of the meaning of people in terms of their lives; the patterns had to be authentic. I liked Dreiser, early Sinclair Lewis, O'Neill, and later, Steinbeck—especially Dreiser. Zola I found too exciting—he aroused my suspicions on this account. I didn't mind sentimentality, but I hated 'thinness', delightfulness, lack of edge, and of mass. I read a lot of Shaw but found myself laughing nastily with him in the thin way my guardian was beginning to laugh at, for example, Mother; though I delighted in his style, I was suspicious of its

rather disqualifying perfection; and his thinking was too
ebullient, too 'sprung' and magical. I preferred immensely Wilde to Shaw, thinking him a truer man. I
read very little poetry, having been put off it at school
where either thundering or 'moved' recitations quite
drowned the sense—poetry should be read, above all,
'sensibly'; the emotion can look after itself; for poetry
lies as much in meaning as in form (the ignorance of
which brings about biases both ways in Shakespeare
production). I was also given a book by a Swedish pastor,
Pfister, on psycho-analysis, which interested me as an
opera might in the mind, encouraging my dramatic
rendering of my own inner life. And the inner life had
come to stay, closing one window after another, for
twenty-five years or more.

In my twelfth year Mother insisted I be confirmed and
accordingly the R.C. priest in the town undertook to
achieve this. He was a pleasant man in an erotic way;
moist eyes, extremely moving voice, gentle manner, and
the kind of self-assurance one meets in a small trite mind
—a small apartment very well furnished. I remember
one day his telling me the story of Christ's birth in such
a way as to reduce me to tears; but the story had the
effect of good fiction splendidly told, and I made no
religious inferences. I began to learn the catechism, and
have never since experienced such embittered boredom,
have never come across such superlatively dogmatic
bilge in print, unless (which it resembles) a popular Press
editorial. My guardian, an atheist of course, was at no
pains to conceal from me the unreasonable demands
Mother was making on me, and that my confirmation
was an essentially formal affair; I had and have no abilities in the conduct of formal affairs, and gave up quickly.

But I can still taste the priest's buttered toast, and his voice.

Towards the end of our five years in the hut (one or perhaps two of which were wintered in the town) my guardian's disposition had been changing, in my opinion for the worse; with alarming symptoms of coquetry and coyness he was talking to women. The furniture dealer's wife, from Clapham, often came down, and I once saw them holding hands in the dim light by the fire; this, I considered to be a complete betrayal of the misogynistic and asocial principles in which I'd been reared. I became increasingly critical of him, thought him stupid and gross and silly, and trembled at the signs of the ridiculous I discovered in him in his awkward attempts at social intercourse—which, to my mystification, were considered 'charming'. In retaliation I acquired a close friend, an Irish woman seeking 'soul' away from her excellent but routine husband (a romanticist in car engines), and, young though I was, I provided this. She gave me an enlargement away from my close life, began to make me see skies and something of normality for a brief time. She was a woman of great charm, of wonderful laughter —the gay Irish kind—lifting my heart with love. She read good books enthusiastically if sentimentally, and my 'intellectual discussions' began their awkward life with her; I truly loved her, not for years having found such freedom, not for years having been able to give play to my childish and at the same time slightly intellectual nature. Our walks with her and her two children were heaven, *jours de fête* in the summer country. Alas that I slammed against her the boulder of my mental cavern, and scowled her graces from my heart, and the sun from my life, as I did again

when my important seventeenth year dawned, rheu-
matically.

My guardian looked like a smudge of unclean fundamentalism by her side; she couldn't win him, because I,
perhaps, had driven him away from all response to a
certain kind of life—the morally rather undressed kind,
which he associated with my family. He was becoming
dingy through excess of principles, and fatuously
sociable.

'The family' had removed to Bayswater. Before an
eventual elevation they had reached rock-bottom in
Chepstow Road, off Westbourne Grove. They were in
two rooms, Mother's and the communal room having
what was left of their furniture and Haslam's being a
combined luggage-room and bedroom; his bed was a
mattress on the floor, from which he rose in the mornings,
grey, malignant, rushing primitively to the teapot—
Mother despised him for being able to drink tea. In his
morning walk he would be dressed in an old grey rain-
coat, sometimes belted with string, and slippers; he wore
a pair of spectacles attached to his ears by string, and was
ruining his eyes on Edgar Wallace and Arnold Bennett
and Sax Rohmer. He no longer believed in his old loves,
and was beginning to acquire a spurious contemporan-
eity which, later, allowed him to use his old true self as a
self-consciously humorous character. The loss of dignity
in this hurt me; I must have had considerable respect
for a certain breadth and dignity in him which compared
favourably with Mother's exacerbated contempt for all
'culture'. And yet in spite of this manifestly sordid life
and apartment Mother's old aroma of *luxe* hadn't gone.
There were still the old scents, silks, coffee, exotic dishes,
peculiar sweetmeats, Virgin Marys, scapulas, crosses

and whatnot, and the immense cabin trunk which porters
on her regular trips to France seemed to have learned to
avoid; her tips were shamefully small, and her luggage—
for she travelled with all kitchen utensils as well as some
heavy religious statues—shamelessly heavy. And though
materially I was living on a superior scale with my guardian, nevertheless there developed apace a feeling of
gaucheness and uncouthness in her presence; she was
slowly taking on the appearance of a 'lady' to me; and the
extra emotional fluency I felt at home with her made going
back to my guardian particularly depressing, though I
disguised this to myself by listening to his moral strictures against her, and to his conviction that she was
'mad'. But I was happy when we sat down to our chess
games, although Mother was a bad loser, sometimes spil-
ling the pieces off the board. And sometimes we had our
special 'luxuries'—chocolate liqueurs beside our black
coffee and Mother with a rare Turkish cigarette; her
favourites were fat ones made by Hadjyani-Vuccino,
some of the best Turkish I've tasted. There was a
tremendous thrill in enjoying sensory pleasures without
English and Protestant awkwardness, and this was partly
responsible for my eventual reaction against my guardian's austere and dim world. She would treat me like
the son of heaven, bringing me delicious omelets for
breakfast with bated breath in case her cooking was
inadequate; omelets, spaghetti and curry were now her
staple diet—with our old French coffee-pot in the family
from time immemorial, with its bashed-in spout and
detachable handle filling the air with its wonderful, past-
haunted aroma. After the initial awkwardness, I knew
peace with her; her anxiety to please me was hard to
endure, provoking brutal movements on my part to keep

her at a distance, for I was frightened of a too close prox-
imity which she always threatened, as later, similar
approaches from women similarly affected me. I was
becoming frightened of the woman nature, with its
power to dissolve sturdy 'masculine' shells, its turning of
one's consciousness to something soft and floundering,
its potential enlargement of the anchorite's trite world.

She too was not unaware of what my sister called my
'commonness'; she would correct my accent and my
behaviour, while I laughed at her peculiar pronunciation
of some words—she said 'years' for ears, and gave long
a's to 'Atlantic' and 'circumstance'. When she wished
to swear she'd say 'buddy'; her baby language was increasing, and she'd refer to herself as 'Thommy-sister'
(her maiden name had been Rodyk-Thompson). She
spoke of herself as a little girl of about five, to whom
incomprehensible things happened; and she laughed
with a little girl's malice and acuteness at my guardian,
and always at Uncle Haslam who more than ever had
become 'Jacko' and 'Poor Bobby Bingo', saying more
than ever that she'd 'got the lot' (in reference to the now
fourteen-year-old bank case—the tin box had disappeared). Having certainly helped his reduction to his
present plight by squashing whatever little initiative he'd
had, she'd mock the results with biting sarcasm; she'd
bid the world 'look at you, unshaven, filthy, useless'.
He'd natter back in furious undertones, frightened lest
she should hear his frequently obscene apostrophes; yet
he made no move and showed no desire to leave her. It
was with some understanding and relish that I read
Strindberg's *The Father* some years later.

He became very jealous of me when I came home for
week-ends; I sympathised with his criticism of my subur-

ban respectability and woodenness. And here he was with Mother who frequently told me it was a pity I should go to such an inferior school, Stonyhurst and Downside being the family favoured establishment to which, she said, if she'd had her way, I would have gone. She even spoke of my entering the Church (the late Bishop Amigo of Southwark was a relative of Father's) or, failing that, the bar; I wished to enter nothing, and to get out of a great deal; if I'd any idea at all of my future it was in the theatre; I was mad about acting, finding myself in that independent of my confusing circumstances and through independence, my meretricious identities. At fourteen I spent six months at Italia Conti's School, after school hours, but was dismayed by the spectacle of excessively refined, girlish boys enacting *Journey's End*.

At school I'd begun a love affair with 'Shirt'. She was plainly pretty, with pinkish skin, small but very ardent blue eyes, and much simplicity rather spoiled with High School hoydenishness—she pretended to be, or she may even have been, devoted to hockey. We pressed hard against each other; I planned every week her undoing—we met on a bench in the playing fields of her little town—but was as timid as a mouse and most uncomfortably exalted, in the Tennysonian way, as my due reward for timidity. I affected in further compensation a saintly disgust with the sexual act—there was, of course, no question of our trying it (at fourteen) yet I behaved as though she were suggesting these favours and I was spurning them like an anchorite. I kept about forty of her letters; the writing squarish with secret roundness, like her character, and very clear, and very dull the letters were: yet potentially pregnant. I sometimes secretly objected to her slightly dampish skin; and she often had pimples. But her legs seemed nice; I never dared carry out my plotted inspection of them; she thought them very private, and kept her skirt down when crossing stiles. She loved her father but not her stepmother and I agreed when I heard the latter's voice. I think I have always known women who loved their fathers very much. My shyness made my substitute role acceptable to me, and satisfied incestuous proclivities. We 'loved' for three years in vain; I liked the vanity of it, religiously: great rapture accrued to me from failing in many an amatory pursuit, and my first set the tone for this. I knew well the religious steam arising from repression, and contrived 'interesting' characteristics out of it, in imitation of my guardian who was similarly dowered; as a result for a long time satisfaction was death in the aftermath. But truthfully when I was satisfied it was the great size of the world that dismayed me; repression kept me in a cosy cupboard. I increasingly inhabited this vast space of dismayingly exact contours with balloons of memory inflated by repressed sex, to bend it to my 'will', conducive to my will-lessness. At school I had begun drawing faces that alternated between dead 'nobility' and lively monstrousness; my own character was in accord.

A mature depression was setting in at fourteen or earlier; a distaste for all that was deemed 'normal'. A fit setting for this I found in Raynes Park and Wimbledon where we moved in 1930.

CHAPTER EIGHT

We moved to Raynes Park because my guardian said he would like to go back to what he called civilisation. He'd begun to find the nightly climb up the hill too exhausting; one evening in the pouring rain he had climbed up on crutches, his leg having broken down and been left behind at Roehampton.

Raynes Park appeared to be a wet suburb; we were near the railway bridge in a tiny, insubstantial house illuminated at night with bulbs of very low wattage. Everything was small, insubstantial and meagre, and the air, after the hill's, likewise meagre and soft, making me tired and excited together. But I smelt with naïve soul the relative sin of town as I'd done on my few excursions to it to meet my guardian in London, at his office. There was nothing to contradict his principles in the apparently co-operative expanses of heath, hill and clouds; whereas in the town I couldn't locate an abiding place for them. The voices jangled horribly, there were too many too-desperate-looking people; and the dreariness of the suburban streets, the 'Avenues' and 'Parades' and 'Walks' suggested 'decadence' as the only possible alternative. But if it became difficult to believe in these principles here, our next move produced conscious revolt. We went to the solider mediocrity of lower-middle-class Wimbledon, the Queen of the Suburbs; a matronly borough, flabby and vulgar, wherein the true opposing principle of all my Mother was to me was soundly established, and which quickened in me the seeds of revolt against my guardian's life-way. Almost overnight a strangely libidinous riot seems to have occurred in my head and heart, and the beginning of the end of my youthful attempts to accept without question my guardian's principles. I sensed adjacent realms of exciting fantasy, irrationality, to which the passport was a developing cerebral excitement. The first signs of my incipient surrealism in life was a sinful jauntiness of demeanour, longer and longer sojourns in what I imagined was the dark consciousness my now favourite author —D. H. Lawrence—preached; and I understood what he meant. I oscillated more violently between cold baths and saintliness and masturbation and D. H. Lawrence, with bouts of film-romanticism in between. I used strong tea and my first cigarettes as agents of my increasing debauch.

My guardian was slowly turning to communism; when I was sixteen he joined the party at Wimbledon (I believe he has long since repented) and showed great courage in taking part in demonstrations and meetings despite the risk of losing his job as a Civil Servant. He did this with a self-abnegation—because he was, in fact, ill-suited personally for gregarious struggle—and that made me cry for him; he was a soundly brave man, much braver than I—but this means little. He was a communist from his heart, from his inverted snobbery and from his loneliness; his brain lumbered painfully after his emotions. Communism, moreover, allowed him to be his simple, rather non-competitive, comradely self; socially he fitted in well with the others. Perhaps he found in it something that he'd mistakenly expected to find in me when he adopted me. From that new standpoint, anyway, he looked critically at me; I felt in very rare moments that his steady criticism of me was more valid than my shrill, neurasthenic criticism of him. But the need to leave him made it impossible to admit this—I had to build him up into a stupid tyrant in order to have something worthy of leaving. This process must have been my first real failure, or the first really noticeable one. I took what I deemed to be the flashy road of 'brilliance', which led to the strange district called 'Fitzrovia', in contradistinction to his of dull integrity. It was, incidentally, the best of what must be called his 'conservative' feelings—for order, decency, human control of fate—that led him to communism. But at first I followed him. I felt he was right; and though I may have changed my practice I have not changed my opinion.

The communists in Wimbledon were 'ordinary people'. There was a Civil Servant, with a family of four and very poor; he was an Irishman with a high red brow, and intensely serious air when talking about himself, but humorous, warm eyes, very large and brown. He worshipped culture, had a very big library for one of his means, and had read most of it. He made understatements with a mannerism that lent them great significance. He once said to me, 'A man doesn't keep his sex life up his sleeve'; people were then beginning to. He was an autocrat among his children, frightened, I think, of his slatternly wife, who was on most occasions very obedient to him, but in an unsatisfied way, which was the way also of his autocratism. He had the extra softness of little men who will pompously select some object or person to admire in order to cover up, by that kind of indirect acknowledgement, a quality they are ashamed of in themselves: also being short and slight he admired my guardian, who was a foot higher than he, and contrasting-ly slow and deliberate in his behaviour (which, I knew, was the cultivated covering for an equal unsureness). At the meetings he enjoyed officialdom, keeping the minutes and making orders of procedure, to his great satisfaction; I pictured him doing the opposite in his office. Nevertheless his 'communism' sprang from his true Irish, rather religious nobility of feeling; he was an ancient idealist of more than one generation's making, and had been—still was probably—humiliated by a life different from his expectations. He had not as much courage as my guardian, usually and understandably pleading the number of his dependents as an excuse from attending demonstrations too openly. But he had integ-rity, and would probably have revealed it in a crisis. I used to play chess with him; he would listen to my argu-ments, which then were beginning to be Nietzschean, with an irony a little beyond his means. Like the majority of party-members, he placed great stress on emotional factors of being a revolutionary: they admitted the science of the dialectical materialist viewpoint, but were emotionally more dedicated than scientifically enlight-ened. They depended, perhaps, somewhat on the mas-siveness of the opposition to provide them with the nice humours of martyrdom and also with a somewhat flippant optimism. The phrase 'The crisis in world capitalism' occurs constantly from the 1920's to our own day; it's easy to point out now that they didn't anticipate the duration of this crisis; they, too, were contaminated by the heady, neo-romantic attitude of 'waiting for the end'. But they had an absolute monopoly of the integumented sense of integrity, intelligence, moral rightness, courage.

Another member was a bus-driver with a fine tenor voice who sang to my guardian's accompaniment; he was a dark-browed, philosophical fellow, excellently balanced, very honest, charming, gentle, qualities he shared with the altogether more mature other members from the working-class proper, of which there were very few in the branch. The majority—of the lower-middle— were certainly subservient to these; there was an element of competition. By drawing to themselves the stigma of being 'intellectuals' they found secretly an enhancement of their attainments, not quite justified and difficult to find elsewhere. They would look shy, a little guilty, but much more vain. They were, of course, much the more extremist in their propositions, but not as able in the practical work. This, of an incredibly dull kind to the unconvinced, was done methodically and capably best by the two or three working-class members, who rarely missed a meeting, and who—slowly but surely—could sustain an argument for much longer and, it was found, more fruitfully, than their erratic social-superiors; the violence of the convictions of the latter served as good blinkers to an untoward understanding. I gained a strong impression of this sample of the 'working-class mind'— mine was already of the splenetic lower-middle kind. Their slowness was beyond my belief, forcing me impatiently into spectacular errors. But their sureness was majestic; here, however, they were apt to sentimentalise a little on arrival, dressing themselves, taking a wash and shave and brush-up at every step of enlightenment, treating themselves rather self-consciously like children on a guided tour of the temple. Nevertheless, the actual progress of their physiognomically demonstrated understanding was as good as a good sunrise, as good as intelligent

children with the extra undertones of emotional understanding and experience. To see and understand them
was a clue to what one had heard of Lenin; one glimpsed
the limitless power of the kind of understanding which
satiated itself with every stage of development, and
invincibly moved to the next bringing with it the whole
machinery of action. To move with body and soul
entire cannot but be spectacular; it is the most impressive view of people. Long after, the memory of them
pointed clearly to what I lacked in myself. I had a glimpse
of this unity raised to a higher intellectual level—and
with a 'spirituality' of saintliness—in hearing Mr.
Saklatvala at one meeting. He was gentle, succinct,
brave, illuminated and illuminating, accurate without
pedantry or brutality, a man one could call, also, un-
conquerable. He suggested the patience of ultimate
victory. I don't know his social origins, but his kind of
mind and behaviour was nearer to that of the working-
class that that of the rest: as, I tended to think, were
those of all men of genius whatsoever.

This level of life was beyond me as soon as I met it,
but I wouldn't admit it. It inspired me—to bright cheap-
ness; but it convinced me of its worth forever. I have not
met it outside the Communist Party; other sincerities
seemed to bury their heads in 'faith' and 'fate'.

But such a level was beyond me for a variety of reasons,
some of which I think I know. For one thing, I was
uncertain in so vulgar a way as to need applause for
everything I said and thought; I could not tolerate the
idea that my 'brilliance', for so I increasingly thought of
myself, being swallowed for no reward but virtue's into
a mass-movement. Intellectually I had the attitude to the
public of a music-hall entertainer. I must get my rabbits

out deftly, and get fame in return; a characteristic that
steadily cheapened and vulgarised everything I attempted. Then, I was a chronic physical coward, terrified of
brutality, policemen, authorities and dogs. Then also,
these and other qualities added up to an aloofness, a
petty-bourgeois parochialism and, really, competitive-
ness that made me wish to monopolise and sell. My
tastes were beginning to be 'unhealthy': snatches of
Nietzsche, whom I was to know better later, and D. H.
Lawrence; the latter became obsessional. The mental
aberration, also, of 'Messianism' was a strong undercurrent in my make-up. I was mad to be acclaimed right;
how wrong I must have felt can be imagined. So, with
the clear sense of going into the night, quite Céline
fashion but with, at least, less bravura and less inverted
'faith'—I edged away from the comrades.

I'd been taking the cinema like a drug in increasing
doses since I was twelve, finding there unconsciousness
in the mental parts and immense fluency of the rest. I
admired the clothes and easy, effective manners of the
moronic heroes; I imitated their faces in the mirror, and
sustained the feeling I took from them of immense
sophistication and general prowess while I walked abroad.
It was a culture for the most part concerned with the
formation of attitudes; films provided fare that were the
familiar romanticism of the lower-middle class, which
my experience, against my will, tried to make my own.
Culture was my church and films were my pub; they
didn't meet, though I filled my time with theories and
ways of their doing so. While I wanted cars and women—
at sixteen—I also wanted the fashionable qualities advertised by the period's novels: integrity, aestheticism,
purity. But perhaps these aspirations were not opposed,

my view of integrity and so on being mental symbols of the cars. I knew that the communists had the clue: they scorned neither, but said the individual getting of them was impossible. I wanted to do alone what they said society must do together. In a word I was greedy. I was congested with desires over which I drew a public face of mourning and asceticism. Privately, I expressed both sets of desires in alternating personalities that didn't bother to meet.

The philosophical sum of the war-novels I'd earlier favoured was nil or pacifist. Of the rest, Aldous Huxley amused me towards nihilism and the excitement and fraternities of 'bohemianism', Lawrence abetted my Christ identification, Nietzsche and Blake (misunderstood)—abetted my antipathy for society. All the qualities of the petty-bourgeois stood out in me clearly and in the extreme. I clung to a feeling of constant loafing, waywardness, which I called 'freedom'; I'd be tied to nothing: neither to people nor ideas, and as little as possible, I imagined, to the world. So I sought what I had enough of already, ignorance, and unconsciousness: filtering into me was the increasingly popular idea that 'subconscious' behaviour was 'greater', of greater significance than conscious behaviour. I deemed it a pregnant liberty.

I developed also a great dishonesty in my reading. I would scamper through books of which I hadn't the least understanding, and then discuss them with that kind of blackmailing omniscience that dares the other person to supply the omissions pointing to my incomprehension. I cannot remember the scientific and philosophical books I was reading, because of this manner of reading them.

Generally, I was beginning to feel great, in inverse proportion to my evident successes. I had been somewhat brought up to believe in the superiority of worldly failure; the bait was fat and I was a simple fish. (This, by the way, in no way implies that I now believe in the superiority of worldly success). I was steadily going mad over myself. Privately, I would prance into the most furious 'war-dances', impassioning myself to a jungle rhythm, then shriek with laughter nicely maniacal, and unfortunately sincere—perhaps in appreciation of my powers of self-deception.

My sister was more straightforward now. She had graduated on the Black Bottom, the Charleston, Benny Goodman, Ellington, Charlie Kunz, the Gargoyle Club; she liked her men to be silken beasts with sentimental ways, and was so herself; she expected nothing of the decency that I affected to want mostly for my own convenience. Her sense of reality was narrow but sharp; a jungle in which she danced. She reduced me almost to piety. I wore my intellect like a modish hat before her; she was slightly impressed, which made me think little of her for I, to tell the truth, was not. My misery was genuine; at fourteen I put my head in the gas-oven—on a pillow; but it was not merely theatrical.

I seemed to walk swathed in the damp cotton-wool of painfully bought sensitivity. Every *moue* of my face was an achievement. I was buying advertisements of a rare soul visible to all, saving up for the misanthropic scowl which, when I eventually bought it, wouldn't go. But certainly I was genuinely hiding something in these grotesqueries—a profound malajustment. So, I became unable to bear the salivated munching of my guardian at meals—he ate auto-intoxicatingly; his three coughs before launching a single dull word were like nails in the coffin of my spirit. I became as vicious as a cat. I fought him continuously and made myself unbearable, mocking everything he said.

My fellow-conspirator against 'suburbia' was one of its fruitiest products. I don't think it's well realized that modes originating in the capital subsist a long while in the suburbs and provinces. My friend was neo-Wilde— true, the time-lapse was only forty years; but his recreation was elaborate, and done with dingy sparkle. He lived on his mother most of the time, finding work degrading. He was ardently homosexual, in the mystical way also, speaking of strange sins in a vintage manner. He revealed a rare psychic anguish over his sexual peculiarity every minute of the day. Every now and then he adorned himself in his own conception of the proper appearance for one of his faith; a cloak or cape, a sombrero, and much ill-applied cosmetic; having a long, horsy, indelicate face, the result wasn't attractive; his heart was very soft, and I think his mother dearly loved him. I imagined a conventional little old lady out of whose entwining arms he could only scoundrelise his way, for he was proud of sin as only the dully virtuous can be. Strangely, he belonged for a short while to the Communist Party—though he was thinking of getting out when I knew him. He did this to his own satisfaction by painting his face at a party meeting and insulting everyone. He was extremely innocent, of course, and worked hard at appearing the opposite. When I met him years later I saw he'd almost achieved his objective, yet not quite. He was become horsy enough, somewhat sinister, his face rumpled, rather like Charles II's, to suggest more vice, probably, than he could fairly lay claim to; but his eyes were as sad as ever, and as simple, and he hadn't lost his pleasant dinginess which his peacock self-presentation so well set off. He wrote tepid verse. He and I preened ourselves in the purlieus, and with each other to each other; he came to see me often.

The strivings of the ill-educated are painful, the outcome usually dishonest: for imperceptibly they aim at and acquire instead of culture, the manners (including, and especially the intellectual manners) of the educated classes. The most general quality in so-called 'working-class writing', at least of the self-consciously such, is dull gentility, caution and wooden complexity of construction; paradox is favoured also. It is the hardest thing in our society to bring the culture of the minority to the intellectual uses of the majority without killing it in wooden formalism: surrealism mistook its nihilism for progress in this direction. But the mistake of the working-class intellectual lies in taking too much, not too little. He may feel that so much is waste, the chaff of manners which long ago was corn, but he rarely dare practise his intuition. I was led into the most pathetic inflations (from which the reader will see that I'm not free) through aping the manners of the cultured classes as I saw them and impossibly their economic and social circumstances; these were, in any case, not truly adjusted to their culture—at the most advanced their culture described the ravages that their social circumstances had made, which were not for my usage; yet I persisted in associating myself with an haute-bourgeoisie crumbling in (to my eyes) romantic dissolution. I had, and have, a depth of snobbery, a fear of working-class people (and my circumstances are below theirs in fact) that I cannot eradicate. It is fear thinly disguised as snobbery, though the foundations of that cannot be much other than fear seasoned with ambition and the guilt of it. I feel that I might be 'lost' in them, that I would lose some precious discrimination; logically convinced that I am, however, of the opposite persuasion, I cannot apply my conviction. Yet nothing's more foolish, and moreover intellectually uneconomical than to separate oneself from one's economic equals: one misses the few advantages of one's economic condition, all of which flower in the recognition of that necessity. This separation was my tower, not even of ivory, but of far memories, associations and weakening pre-dispositions.

One morning I 'had a funny feeling' on the platform of the station waiting for my train to school. When it came in I looked at it merely, detaching myself from the inevitability of getting in it. I did this successfully; it went out slowly and normally, leaving me behind. I crossed to the other platform and took the train to Waterloo and my mother, having decided no more to go to school. Mother looked a little embarrassed, but pleased. She didn't question my right to leave school when I wanted. I stayed a while with her until my guardian heard.

When I left school thus voluntarily my guardian was of course very angry. For the first and only time he spoke to me of careers; he said he'd intended to send me to a university (I had failed twice to matriculate) and later to the bar; before then—but not even then was I much clearer—I had known nothing of why one went to school. It was done on faith and compulsion. I had little of the former, and intended to suffer as little of the latter, its discreetly common form.

He told me I should get a job; I told him I would write. So he said he would keep me for a year; I took a room in the town I'd been to school in and began a book, when I was seventeen—the first version of this 'confession'. I called my book *Sean and the O'Neils*, and made it a spectacular account of my sufferings with much about the dark consciousness in it: for I was now in the full swing of my Lawrence period, though it was years later in great intoxications that I'd write on lavatory walls, 'the great unconscious is divine' (which is as near to a belief in God as I've reached). I lived very frugally, in the house wherein my English schoolmistress also lived; she took a grand interest in my 'talent' and in my dawning vagabondage, delighting to drive me on to the heath and drop me there with a bar of chocolate for the night. I worked hard, chilled to the bone, in saluting a literary dawn and felt so ashamed of my evident failure that I persisted in the attempt for many many years. I finished my book before the year was out and took it to an agent, who said it was promising, advised me to rewrite certain passages and make more of my mother whom she called the most interesting 'character'. I didn't care to see Mother interesting, and threw the manuscript away.

Meanwhile, Mother had become seriously ill; I learned the pains she'd suffered for ten years were caused by cancer in the womb. She was taken to St. George's Hospital but, faithful to her contempt for her husband's profession, refused to be operated on. She was then returned to her flat in the Cork Street basement, where she'd been for some months. In the hospital, in a private room, she told me she was getting better; she was quite childlike, and her eyes were huge and dark beneath, her body, reduced from its past plumpness, become emaciated, her hands little claws and her cheeks hollow. It was difficult for me to hear what she said.

I stayed with the family in Cork Street for the few days until she died. The night before, we seemed at last to be in love. It was the first time I had been so frankly and so unconventionally with anyone for years, and was astonished, dimly, at all I'd thought and said against her; most of these things happened far away from my consciousness; there, I was in a trance of attention to the few things she said—that I should, for instance, be famous as a gipsy had told her, and that she didn't mind dying, and would see the Virgin Mary, she hoped. Uncle Haslam was hopeless with misery, evidently robbed of the most important person in his life. He stood at the end of her bed waiting for her to want anything; she looked kindly at him now, and died in his arms. He was very kind to me afterwards, and seemed oddly to have an agreement with my refusal to go to the funeral.

Her last expression was one of a dawning realisation of some shape in her life, one of beginning to understand what had been confusion; I saw the same in the eyes of Dolores Costello in her death scene in the *Magnificent Ambersons*.

Mother's death made my rootlessness, my isolation, my desperation sensible to me. I assumed, without realisation, that I'd made a mistake, and that I belonged to her world and not to my guardian's; her last expression had not been one of wickedness, madness, irresponsibility, but had been reasonable, serene, and then understanding, and also clear; my guardian's ways became muddy to me. Alive, I had gone through the perfunctory motions of casting her off without knowing what I was doing; dead, my isolation began to live with her; I seized hold of what I knew now her heart had been, and allowed in myself a resurgence of the old spontaneity I'd had with her; an upgush that led me to fantasy, but also led me to express my confusion, which proved cathartic.

As a final remark upon her, I'd say she was a woman whose natural equanimity, civilisation of heart and, I fear, breeding, failed to make head or tail of this most vulgar of imaginable worlds. She dismissed it quickly, and reverted to illusions of childhood, finding some happiness in them—more than my 'rational' guardian would have allowed her; and this virtue of the heart she had is the great virtue.

I left my room where I'd struggled with *Sean and the O'Neils* and took one in Putney by the river, living on the twenty-five shillings my guardian continued to allow me; I was nearly eighteen. And here, on endless rolls of shelf paper, I wrote my philosophy, which I called *Interjectivity* and which propounded the unity of the subjective and objective worlds, unfortunately in a terminology created to express their differences; unity and difference I could not then combine, and became so entangled and incoherent that I relaxed in writing verse composed in a private language, a purely phonetic rendering of animal and baby sounds; thus composing, I would reach a point of excitement where my mouth would be drenched with saliva.

Terrors of walking in Putney High Street were encroaching on me rapidly and to pepper myself into a state of greatness sufficient to allay them, I would play over and over *On with the Motley* from Pagliacci; then I would form my jaw into Mussolinian dimensions as I stepped on to the street.

Nearby lived the Irish lady whom I'd known on the hill. I spent as much time as possible with her, making literary talk while I helped her wash up.

I cut myself off from my connections with the Communist Party after an encounter with a local comrade. He had asked, 'would I save a drowning man at sea?' 'Only if I could swim', I replied; the identical question the Father Superior of a monastery asked me when I attempted to become a monk, to whom I gave the same reply. I had gone to him as a religious seeking a confirmation of my faith, but had switched at the sight of him. To go religiously to communism is the wisest investment in future apostasy, there being no doubt at all that it *was* 'The God' That Failed. Though I cut myself off, I always professed to be a communist, and rarely criticised the party. As an explanation of my inactivity I offered the complexities of my soul, and went out of my way to accuse myself of cowardice and individualism.

Part Two

WAITING FOR THE END

CHAPTER NINE

I met in Putney a poet (Laurie Lee) in a more sober version of my own condition, and with a more practical resolution of its problems. He was working on a building site, as a labourer, in order to save enough money to play his fiddle round Spain. I was at once privately critical of this tritely picturesque programme—for so I esteemed it. He would, I thought, perform that which was serious business, in order to avoid its deeper ramifications. I saw him on the trail of professionalism; I was on that of Christ identification or messianism—the vulgarisation of a core of common enough inquiry. Spain, I thought in connection with the young poet, was an attribute he was off to purchase; he had conditioned himself in advance and was to fill himself with its 'appropriate' experience. His courage, which I slightly admitted, seemed to be based on a dearth of past casualties. His departure made me stick all the more misanthropically to Putney, and gloat over the sombre hues of my dingy state. I idled delightfully, finding often the time heavy, when I'd have to excite myself with tea, Woodbines and Pagliacci; but I relished the freedom to ramble alone at night to town or on Wimbledon Common, where I was pleased to walk with my head thrown right back to give me the sensation of walking in the stars. Stars were my 'Spain', and had the advantage of ubiquity.

I was fully engaged in reading Nietzsche now, my

preferred volumes being the *Will to Power*; and I wept over Zarathustra's exalted solitude. I also read Ulysses. At the same time I sent some verses to Aldous Huxley; he returned them with kindly comments and Mallarmé's precept that poetry was written with words, not feelings. Huxley was a writer who excited me to the appreciation of my precocity but whom I did not at all admire, and I sent the poems in a spirit of vulgar ambition that I much chided myself for. I saw him then, going occasionally to tea, to Albany and his studio over a garage. He walked round me as round an exhibit of some slight interest. While we were walking up Haymarket in a yellow evening fog he appeared to me for a moment as the ideal literary man— a clue to my conception of intellect, as something grubby, something done in a very private kitchen, not divorced quite from alchemy; he was cerebrally exciting. He was tall, wore a wide-brimmed period hat, and remarkably resembled my mother. He was also for me the protagonist of the idea that all one had to do to understand humanity was to look at it—a period fallacy, but one very stimulating to the ego. I saw him several times, but nothing came of it; being closely regarded paralysed me, so that, for instance, in attempting to describe my philosophy to him, I indicated a rectangle and a moving line in it, at right-angles to the base: the line was 'consciousness', the parts either side, the subjective and the objective worlds. I thought his 'bright' characters extremely dull, and wondered how so much knowledge could be satisfied with such two-dimensional people; I was annoyed at the coarseness of his analysis, and more annoyed because it was very good writing. *Point Counter Point* reminded me in content of that which Wyndham Lewis reminded me in style—rocky boulders made of cardboard, but looking like an avalanche of something impressive in the distance.

I again met my homosexual friend from Wimbledon. I refer to his homosexuality, because that was his main and most self-conscious attribute. He took me to a meeting of a 'Psychological Society' in London, my first introduction to Fitzrovia. The society was constituted mainly of homosexuals which did a small but expanding business as a psychic brothel. It was, I suppose, a face-saving device for the respectable elements, who hadn't the courage of their physical appetites, without psychiatric blessing. The studio was filled with the lower class of hard-bitten aesthetes who throbbed and thrived in a Messiah's pronouncements of cryptically smutty words and apocalyptically naïve indecencies. The High Priest of the society was a Captain Grandhomme, a mature medical student on the way to becoming a psychiatrist. His face was softly plump and deadly white, with a small cherry-red, moist mouth; he spoke, in the succulence of wet jams, of the terrible and deep things that lay dormant in the human psyche, in the manner of the Brothers Grimm, whose fairy tales had been my favourites. Once, coming to the meeting alone, I was behind him at the front door and he turned round with a feminine yelp, high-pitched and called me another name; he looked at me closely, and seemed to take at once an interest in me. He lectured like a soft fondant from the depths of a tobacco-coloured arm-chair, the light arranged with artful discretion above his head. Practically all the society were being analysed at the time, and analysed each other as well. Many of them were painters, in styles deriving from Dufy, Utrillo, Rouault. The theme of their painting was invariably the magic of something 'purely' revealed;

it hung like a dripping gobbet on their canvases, and reflected their own self-conceptual revelation. They believed in the utmost freedom, but chiefly on the sexual plane with the aesthetic one for what couldn't be used up on the sexual. They were elaborately and religiously 'sexual'. It was my first introduction to 'the dark consciousness' in action, though I didn't immediately make the connection. The Messiah and his Priest had gathered their goods from Freud, Jung and India; they had travelled for a year in that land for suburban English revelation and brought home the brightly made articles of their faith.

One effect of attending a few meetings—I scoffed with a little fascination—was an increment in my tedious self-analysis. I saw phallic shapes as phalluses; later attempted to see phalluses as architectural shapes (chimney-pots, etc.). But the enlightenment bored me; I hadn't quite their experience of repression; they were all respectable people, and ran their lives competently outside this 'pub'. Moreover, since I'd heard of Freud I was violently prejudiced against the sexual interpretations of actions, opposing to them an inadequately understood social interpretation.

There were a few unwilling old ladies with iron grey hair, who were on a fox-hunt for sex their artful dodger, lesbians, masturbators, homosexuals, sadists and masochists, of course. I was susceptible enough to the environment (which the society was also encouraging) to take a dive further into 'unconsciousness', or automatism. The eventual common result of this way was, of course, the flattest conservatism. But I liked the painting atmosphere, and had begun myself to paint appallingly.

A little better, and infinitely more elaborately organised than the thought of the society was the surrealist movement, now percolating through to London. I was becoming interested in it, for, among other advantages, it condoned my very apparent lack of technique in verse and paint. In fact I found most of my weaknesses as considered adornments by the movement. Later, on seeing a group of surrealist 'leaders' in a photograph taken on the occasion of the Burlington Gallery exhibition, I thought how straightforwardly criminal, from pickpocket-ish to murderous, they all looked. I have rarely seen a more furtive group of faces; but for long I esteemed what I still think to have been the cathartic value of the movement. I particularly took to Dali's theory of paranoiac criticism; it was my only kind. The movement condoned, as I've suggested, my way of life. I became a conscientious irrationalist, and indeed graduated to a nerve hospital soon after.

However, my freedom was temporarily curtailed by my guardian's stopping my allowance. He disapproved of my 'life' and proceeded to wash his hands of me. He had come to regard my sister as sensible. A change had come about since mother's death. Haslam slowly threw off her domination and had revealed unsuspected abilities as well as vulgarities; he smirked more, with self-esteem, and became cleaner, and eventually the editor of a health magazine. My sister had also hardened; she and Haslam were completely in accord, in a conspiracy to establish themselves more favourably in the world. Haslam gave his fatherly authority to her various love affairs, and in return she trotted him out to her lovers and friends as a witty and venerable old 'character', a part he played disgustingly well, toning down his old asperity and misanthropy and, really, making a joke of all he had been. He had been something of a genuine misfit, and he now became a fraudulent conformist: the virtue of the family, and the failure as well, had gone with mother. And I as her surviving representative—for I was very like her, in my life as well as character—was to be corrected and coerced into the ways of decency; the battle being joined, I had no doubt of my own victory. But the battle was severe. I became my sister's servant more or less, washing up and cleaning in return for a room and food—though I believe my guardian contributed a little towards my upkeep. I too was trotted out as a freak in suitable company. But since I adhered to the roots of my oddness I made a poorer show of it than Haslam. My hatred for my sister developed apace. My only defence was the cultivation of a clumsy and incompetent aestheticism which grated on me more than on her, for it was formed to her standards in the matter. I remember once in the middle of pummelling a piece of clay in my bare room (with just a mattress on the floor) being called out to 'meet', as a curiosity, one of her more brittle friends; I shouted in a frenzy that they cared nothing for the truth and were horrible people. This so suddenly split the thin skin of my sister's not yet matured sophistication that the silence was informative to me. Having said more than I meant to say, I found what I meant. But unfortunately I laid too large claims to that disputed 'truth'. I was to carry it around like a large log.

Sometimes while washing up I lost sight of the water and traced lines and circles in the suds, and then the lines would be a road I had walked along with my mother in Wimereux. I was happy when I could dream, in any way whatever. I stayed in the kitchen as much as possible.

As in time I appeared quietly to adapt myself—which

displeased my sister as much as the opposite, for she wanted me, of course, to get a job—inwardly I was breeding a tigerish determination to go. One morning I broke open her gas-meter and went off with the proceeds. I determined to be a tramp, for I had very much liked wandering through London by the hour. I made for the Surrey hills, then to Winchester, Portsmouth, Plymouth; I wrote to a friend of mine asking him to send me six shillings a week, which he did; then I continued north. I slept out in haystacks, sometimes in barns, felt very wretched and hungry but had no thought of returning. I met a tramp in Lancashire pushing a pram with a gramophone in it, and I collected the pennies for him one evening while he played hymns. He was an old fellow of sixty, apple-cheeked, tiny and gay. At night in his tent he made sexual overtures, and not wishing to offend him, or rather hurt him, I attempted to comply, but the machinery was not suitable. Next morning he asked me if I thought him pretty; I said, certainly. I kissed him good-bye. This cheered me—the human feeling, I mean. At the beginning of October it was getting cold, and reaching some big town in the north, I wrote to Haslam asking him to send me the fare home. But when it reached me I changed my mind and took the boat to Eire.

Walking had a saddening but soothing effect on me. I had always preferred the country to the town; I liked roads and moving, like my mother. I liked being without the bother of dressing and washing, and I liked very much the absence of the gymnastics of 'social life'. I felt 'the truth' would come, too. Tramps here and there were very nice to me. I thought them very pleasant people, having reached through resignation an unusual kind of maturity; mentally they were what's called subnormal,

WAITING FOR THE END

but in another way, far more dignified than the settled
men. Perhaps because the hiatus between their material
desires and their satisfactions was so immense, that that
between thought and speech was very short; I could feel
more normal with them because I, too, hadn't learned the
civilised customs-house between the two. Moreover I
had an emotion similar to their doggy surliness when
they spoke to strangers, restful after my sister's display
of wanton hospitality shown to her friends; I'd been in
an agony of conviction as to her 'hypocrisy', so that
speaking to her made me furiously entangled in her
decent inability either to understand or reply in my own
terms. Today this 'hypocrisy' has become clearer to me
in people; I mean, I can see something of its origin and
its protective function and, as with many other qualities
of people I saw, imaginedly or not, with dismay at this
time, I can attempt to understand their systematic con-
ditioning by society; the individual no longer seems
'guilty' but the group does. I was, of course, suffering
from a serious acceptance of the attitude inculcated at
school—that people make themselves; how else, I
thought, could they be responsible for themselves?
Whereas, of course, responsibility, being impossible
among an anarchy of individuals, is mere blackmail to
conformity. And this attitude was basically responsible
for my maladjustment.

Moreover tramps were spattered with the road, with
the roughness of sleeping out, with the spiritual *finesse*
hidden within the grossness arising from lack of employment; their eyes were wild, darting, aimed directly by
the purposive intelligence, and there hovered nothing
about them of that greasy, insulating caution of expression, tartiness of behaviour, meanness of gesture,

incumbent upon hard workers for their daily bread; none of that vice which comes from servants of unelected masters, none also of that self-dissolvent, messy intimacy of their close relationships. The 'I' of a tramp was dirty, gnarled, but tough, no lady, but fundamental to the human race.

I was moved and thrilled too by their smell of distance and space, one of the greatest spiritual elegancies available to man, which polishes him like a knife. One man under his sky is an eternal image, however lapsing it may be from the 'progressive social consciousness'; this is most beautifully, if most errantly, expressed by Nietzsche, and an incomparably greater image than that of the dreary soul doing its farce of solitude in its body's armchair.

But in Dublin, after drifting around the quays and finding the air very beautiful and the Liffey very kind and unreal, and the Irish also (reality had become British to me), I panicked. Alone on the roads I felt quiet and secure in what I was doing; an obvious thing to do, to wander away to look at things and not to be bothered with an alien-feeling circus of affairs. But in a town, even one like Dublin, I hadn't the confidence to resist the opposite view; I half felt I was mad, and cunningly thought I could certainly pass for it and thereby get food and shelter for a while. So I applied as a prospective lunatic to the mental hospital, but the doctor rejected my claims. I spent a night in the workhouse to which I went accompanied by a gang of gentle loafers who got blind drunk in a whisky shop before climbing the hill back. In the morning I shovelled stones into a cart for three hours. But the porridge was very good, and the place cleaner and more proper than those of the same kind I've been in over here. I then tried the Salvation Army shelter which I thought would demand credentials of respectability. So I described my wanderings as the vagaries of a comfortably-off eccentric, the dreaming kind. They wrote to Haslam who sent the fare for me to come home. I found the shelter pleasant enough, the officers extremely class-conscious, and the inmates utterly contemptuous of them. An officer was to have met me at Waterloo but I dodged him. When I reached my sister's, Haslam and she and I at once debated whether I should be sent to a Borstal. But this was a threat, not an intention, and I stayed a while forgiven.

However, things were no better. My self-esteem had been augmented by my five-months tramp; I returned to the psychological society, and met again the Captain Grandhomme I've mentioned. He took a great and flattering and slightly frightening interest in me. He asked me if I would like to stay in Cambridge with him the next term; I said I would, and he arranged the matter with my sister. In the taxi going to my sister's I caught an impression of him as an exceedingly lush person, who liked to fume and plume himself out till he lolled fat and glossy, his soul engrossed in tasting the savours his body provided. In his positive activity he seemed thin, rather bad tempered in nervousness. But in his state he glowed like a fat old moon. He was about thirty-eight when I met him, but in appearance jumped from infancy to senility. He was quite a fraud, but as a hysteric, sincere; one could tell that by the vagaries of his voice. He was a very serious, if not an exceptionally accomplished, voluptuary. He liked dressing up in strange robes, and later told me he'd been a priest in the Russian Orthodox Church. His 'mysticism', quite a simple affair, was more in the ritual than the thought;

he saw the 'depths' in almost anyone. Haslam looked odd beside him, as did any man, I noticed: they looked clumsy, and rude; strangely enough so had other men beside my guardian. I liked his atmosphere of careful, but erratically luxurious prosperity which was rather like mother's on a higher level.

It was agreed that I spend four months with him in Cambridge. I had thought my sister would suspect him of homosexuality, which perhaps she did and didn't care. My own ideas were still vague; I hadn't yet distinguished between sexual warmth and affection proper; in those days, anyway, they were colliding, and were thought to be approaching their real identification with each other.

He was of the kind who, like my guardian, ostensibly protected one into a dependence that turned gradually into the emotional opposite. He 'did a baby on one'. He had a word, 'jumbly', for people like, he said, himself, me, my mother, the Messiah of the Society and some of his Cambridge friends. Jumblies didn't grow up. They liked bright things most, and listened to the gong-music, as we did, of other jumblies, such as the Balinese, the Indians. Jumblies cosily must get together to keep the other cold kind of people out, who didn't understand sensuous living, but briskly drilled on the social square. I had to agree that my mother had been a jumbly, and that my sister wasn't and that I had strong tendencies that way. In the taxi going to the station, I immediately felt that I was suffering the misfortune of being taken off by one of my own babyish kind; it was like, terribly like, going off with Mother to France. He released in me what I'd been trying to ignore—a 'social age' of about four. I had thought and thought as much as I could, but had not

grown up at all. Before men I felt so ridiculously infantile as to be frightened of their guessing so. I preferred
women to whom, I discovered, it didn't matter so much.

He rented two attic rooms in a boarding-house in
Cambridge, roughly arranged to the requirements of an
'ashram', as he said. One of his main occupations was in
assemblies of young misfitting men to fish for depths,
which were invariably erotic—depth and profundity
were always erotic. He attended lectures in the mornings
and afternoons; we had meals together with the other
boarders; I remember often looking furtively around to
see if they saw a secret I dimly suspected as being dis-
creditable to Grandhomme and myself; and Grandhomme's manner was essentially cautious and artificial
in public. He ate mystically, carefully breaking small
pieces of Ryvita, drinking water or wine as one might at
communion. He was behaving as a greatly enlightened
person all the time, a man of spiritual importance; I
cannot remember a single significant thing he ever said to
me. He had a small mind, as incapable of reflection as it
was well versed in the strategy of satisfying his desires
through people. He was forced to make much of the
spiritual importance of his physical pleasures, for they
were judged from the elaborate structure he built to
make his sex-life morally acceptable to him. He was a
man of quite vast emptinesses; perhaps they were the
ancestral corridors of his family background (he was
cousin to one of our leading politicians, of an 'illustrious'
family).

One evening Grandhomme sounding particularly
musical to himself, so that his white flesh might have
been the house of a sentimental neurological blues band,
began speaking of Mother. I said at last that she had

frightened me (and knowing the unconscious twist of my mind, I may have meant he frightened me); then I told him of my gorilla nightmares. I was staring into the gas-fire, and saw there suddenly Mother's face perfectly done in the red-hot clay, yellow and blue-gauze flames giving it a vibrating actuality; and then her face changed into the gorilla's, and both—the gorilla head on my mother's body—rolled as off the world back over the top of the flames.

Some nights later I had a nightmare about Grand-homme. The strange man professed to be under the spiritual guidance of a Master (a 'guru'), who lived in the room as a mystically potent painting (done not very well by the Messiah). I had been elaborately prepared for this painting, and saw everything I'd been told to in its Egyptian eyes and its trite symmetry. I jumped up terrified from bed and in slippers and pyjamas and over-coat left the house and found some night-watchmen in a building site. I asked if I could sleep by their fire, which they allowed. Grandhomme was alarmed next morning, as he always was at the danger of his private mumbo-jumbo life becoming known, and what had been the beginning of oblique advances ceased. He kept me there in the spirit of carrying out the letter of his undertaking, while I, wanting something, not quite knowing what, stayed resolutely. Yet the nightwatchmen had reminded me of something that, by staying with Grandhomme, I was in danger of losing—something I'd had with Pierrot and other simpletons of my childhood.

Grandhomme's 'ashram' consisted of five or six students, mostly medical, two of whom were to continue their studies in psychiatry. They were his lovers too; that was the mystery. He was fatherly, or really motherly;

but they rather took him as a passing show. They were young men with something missing in their lives; Grandhomme ably parodied the something, thus training them to dispense with it in the spirit of a workable cynicism. He was good fun for them, but had dangers too, in his hysteria. His favourite word was 'stimulating', with 'profound' a close second ('stimulating' was his highest expression of admiration, like a novel critic's) and 'profound' his term of depressed admiration; he believed in the 'darkness'. Grandhomme was a baby with a cunning trick or two of confusing his elders. He allowed himself to show emotion in public, a rarity in England which alone was enough to make him remarkable. In that he was like Mother—as, indeed, in many ways. He introduced me to drink and to more mature, self-respecting inflations than the desperate ones of my childhood.

Later, Grandhomme became a psychiatrist, and at the death of his mother (to whom he was devoted), he came into quite a lot of money and gave Ranji a life-income. When the war broke out he went to Eire with others of the society; they recommenced operations but came into conflict with the Church which Grandhomme had to explain away, for he admired the Church because of its statues and vestments and incense. He became a noted psychiatrist in Dublin, making a lot of money; but at forty-five he died suddenly of anaemia. He told me at Cambridge one frightening night of his guiding 'psychic image': of himself as a white wolf carrying a dripping piece of meat (his chops flecked with blood) across snow, alone: he was a very hungry man indeed.

The period of my stay ended and I returned to London, but found living at my sister's more irksome than ever; I hung around the Fitzrovia district, and eventually was allowed to sleep in the society's studio. But, as one whom he'd failed to seduce, I was become a nuisance to Grandhomme; he yelped more than ever when he felt me behind him unexpectedly; and an atmosphere of unbalance had been growing around me to which I contributed, for madness was fashionable, and I was proud of my mite.

I liked not to know what to do; I one day took a chair in Hyde Park in the orators' corner and said as much, and other things. I also said Freud should be joined to Marx. I gathered considerable crowds round me, who were only a little less impressed by my babble than I; messianism had come in full swing. Before I spoke I would move ominously through the crowd, feeling the voice growing and swelling within me. Its bigness was suffocating.

I met young men similarly disposed in my audience; an American surrealist who called himself Zion Adamthree but didn't write at all well, two Canadian snuffy intellectuals without money. A coloured postcard was done of me and sold, called *Le Bourgeois sans Souci*. I wore red trousers and bobbed hair, partly because other people didn't, and because I didn't want to be overlooked. Having made sure that I wouldn't be overlooked, I complained heavily of people staring at me.

I met also the first man I had considerable respect for: a rather racketty, but finely drawn, integrated young sculptor called Doon, who was about to leave his art for politics. He had the common sense that wasn't dim; he welded animal spirits to a reasonable approval of his activities, which merited them; I sensed health in him. He was alive but not reckless, feeling no need to advertise his vitality to his own undoing—though somewhat to his own making. He said a memorable thing to me: that I couldn't deceive myself—but he underestimated my powers of attempting to. He was cunning, but not furtively so; he fed well, unlike the rest of us; he exploited and absorbed an environment to the full, then moved on when it became confining. He had an unusually tender sympathy for the less tough than himself; he was *au fait* with animals, of which his drawings (in the Gaudier-Brzescha style) were some of the best I've seen: all his drawing had a feeling of loneliness, and of the pathos of brute strength, which can only be employed for its eventual destruction. His lions were homely-figured creatures; his mandrils were inspired with nobility become a fury. He had a vulgar streak and naturally composed for himself a dreadful contempt for humanity.

I don't know what I lived on during this period; on sixpences, half-crowns, from the society, friends, my sister; I painted water-colours for our local art-dealer and junkman, who paid me 1½d each for them, and up to five shillings for oils. He collected some hundreds of them. For six months I sold an average of a shilling's worth a day.

I felt very much at peace speaking in the Park. Thinking aloud in the open air, even nonsense was very blissful. One evening a girl in the crowd in the Park had edged her way to the front and looked invitingly at me. I spoke to her after the meeting and we became friends. Every evening afterwards I closed the meeting when she appeared. We lived together for a while in a studio of the society's; she was Scotch-Greek, seventeen, sexually insatiable; she took baths, sometimes, with an old man for ten shillings, and bought food. And when we were very short, I would raid my sister's flat, mostly for pots of jam.

It dawned on me slowly that I didn't know where I was—evidently feeling the need to. I was encouraged, I think, by Grandhomme, whom I saw occasionally, to feel peculiar; certainly not discouraged. I felt profound; at street turnings not knowing which way to go—which, really, was most logical, for I had nowhere to go either way. But I insisted on this being 'strange'—and induced a feeling of 'vibrations', as though shattered by opposite tendencies. One day, loaded with my cargo of strangeness, I went in glad full sail to the Messiah and told him. He entered into the spirit of the thing and consulted with Grandhomme; I found myself whisked in a taxi to a nerve hospital for milder mental cases; Grandhomme made an impassioned plea for my admittance to the doctor who said there was a long waiting list. Grandhomme knelt on one knee, and either clasped his hands or put one on his heart, looking more worthy of admission than myself. The doctor agreed to take me. Grandhomme arose with a moist brow. I was scrubbed and put into the observation ward for a fortnight, where on the third day a tall red-faced man next to me died. I relaxed; a proper kind of palace for my kind of monarch.

CHAPTER TEN

I was soon moved into another ward. From a report I came across later (the 'L.C.C. Hospitals Report') I found I'd told the doctor I was willing to be there but that I had no hope of changing. I was classed, I saw in the report, as a schizophrenic, an unusually young one. I think I was their youngest patient.

I affected great unwillingness to speak to other patients at first, and also (rated as a symptom) refused to clean my room when, at my own request, I was moved into one. I viewed the doctors with as much contempt as my features could express; I couldn't believe them capable of understanding me, and certainly didn't want them to; their faces, I thought, showed no 'intuitions', save one—that of a clever young man whom I liked and feared slightly. They appeared to me desperately on the outside of a world they'd give their world to enter; I treated them as unprivileged gate-crashers.

But I liked the place very much, being allowed more or less to do as I pleased, painting, writing and not having to 'work'; and certainly having my psyche seriously considered wasn't, in a coarse way, unflattering; I developed there little frills of manic mystery that it took many years to shed—and still, in fact, hurl ocular depth-charges at innocent skies as a signal of my holy privacy. However, I doubt my behaviour would compare un-favourably with, say, Dr. Graham's, or any rather tired schoolmaster's. The majority of patients were tediously insistent on their perfect normality; the atmosphere was normal, heightened, like a Joos ballet of organised behaviour. One night, I awoke as from a trance, and, in the glare of the Crystal Palace which was burning—we could see it from the veranda where we slept—I caught a snap-glimpse of other patients, some dressed, and felt them, from their clothes mostly, to be thrillingly contemporary, of *today*, absolutely, and I imagined an element of cure in this experience, despite my prevailing scientifically ignorant conception of neurosis as the unemployed, wasted part of imaginative talent.

I was probably a patient here illegally since I was a minor and my guardian hadn't given his consent. I disbelieved in my schizophrenia, considering myself little more than neurotic. But in any case, I found my introspection consolidated and strengthened by the treatment; a direct follow-on from periods of intense recollection of past fixated events—one, for instance, of Jeannette entering the *salle à manger* in Wimereux with a cockerel whose neck she had just wrung—I had sobbed and shrieked. Then, for hours I gabbled Spanish-sounding words from the back of my throat, finding immense satisfaction in it, as in my dreams of singing tenor; my whole body participated. I was treated with Dr. Gutmann's pills, which I was told rebuilt the tissues of the glands; their effect on me was to excite me wonderfully in different parts of my body—in my testicles which encouraged me to masturbate; and when the doctor entered immediately after the event I was scarlet with embarrassment and told him angrily to go away. But I had intense erotic sensations in my throat as well.

I left in six months with the consciousness of having

become a grubby, conventional 'intellectual'; and that a thick glass pane, as is proper to such 'intellectuals', had been fixed between me and the world. I felt no more so excruciatingly involved in my reactions to things, but confined to an office in my brain with the door locked against unseemly exits. I felt old, cynical, department-alised, my mind in its sensory remove from the world working much harder and more consistently, but lacking the original spurts and 'inspirations', and on a thinner diet. In fact, I became the chief object of my attack for years after. I did not wish to return, a pasteurised prodigal, to my sister—and her Argentinian lover whose boils I attributed to her promiscuous chastity—and therefore repaired to my old haunts. In the hospital I'd written a long poem among others, a skit on the popular romantic novel, and an editor interested in the labours of the mad had seen and printed it in his *avant-garde* magazine. I went off to collect the money; the editor said he wasn't in the habit of paying but made an exception in my case. He said he'd judged me to be thirty instead of twenty from the cynicism of the effort (cynicism was regarded as a mature attribute). I was paid thirty shillings for the poem, and for the next three years published regularly in the verse magazines, exciting, I gathered, unreasonable hopes in the editors' breasts of being a 'find'. To me my poems are the mess of my having collided with my head against the brick wall of society's guardians, a shock-spill of sensations and thoughts in surrealist disarray, contemporarily suitable. I spent no longer than the time required to write them out twice, sometimes once—about half an hour on each. They resemble the worst work of the 'thirties, dealing exclusively with 'psycho-sensations' in a strained apocalyptic manner. It astonished me that they were taken 'seriously', but of course I followed suit in my attitude to them—but not to the extent of writing them carefully, for I would then have robbed them of their pristine inaccuracy. They were middle-class concoctions, which I knew and resented, and I expressed my resentment by composing them roughly. Some had lines that weren't bad, inevitably; one funny one went through three anthologies. My aim or desire—I can't say that the desire materialised into an aim—was to write as a communist, in the Mayakovsky manner; but my writing persisted in its 'decadent' manner, beyond my control. I seemed to be living for a while on poetry, which may have been another reason for despising my efforts. They were undoubtedly mountebankery.*

But seeing my name in print frequently encouraged my worst tendencies. I felt less than ever inclined to 'work', regarded myself as a legitimate freak in the surrealist school. I met an Australian painter I'd known who took me to his cottage for a while in Essex; then a poet and his wife, Charles Madge and Kathleen Raine, asked me to stay with them. I here played with stiff conscientiousness at being a poet. Madge and his wife were extremely kind to me, but I just couldn't understand them or feel at home in their world; again my so unprofitable allergy to 'the middle classes' became unbearable; I felt exhausted by their conceptualism which was remote from my own experience of the world—the less comfortable parts of it; I felt I was being 'spiritualised' away and in me this feeling has definite physical manifestations, of breathing through the chest and feeling faint and of an apparent sexual neutralisation.

* Secure in a minority of one, I can now reverse this opinion.

Mass Observation was then being founded at their house,
and I found no interest in it, without being very much
asked to. It was then proposed that I do 'surrealist'
writings on zoo animals; I therefore used to go off on a
bicycle every day to stand in front of the animals and
wait for piquant disarrayed thoughts. But the animals
were not co-operative and the thought that came was one
that bade me cease and walk on. On the other hand, a
vulgarity always on the fringe of me, that I have perpetu-
ally to brush off, made me feel flattered at having an
established, and certainly intelligent poet taking an
interest in me; so much so that I gate-crashed Mr.
Empson's party before his trip to China. My dramatic
egotism did, I thought, have prospects in the company of
people whom I regarded as rabid, if esoteric and subtle,
amateurs of personality—people who narrow-eyedly
scrutinised personality as the wonder of man. But after
three weeks with the Madges I moved to the open-air,
more or less, sleeping sometimes in rooms of friends. I
stayed next to Doon for a while in Brecknock Studios,
with the Australian painter friend, and with them began
to drink experimentally, the hospital pills having given
me a taste for different states of consciousness. With
them, too, I attended a few meetings of the group of
surrealists in Hampstead. The atmosphere was not
unlike Grandhomme's 'ashram' and we would sneer, not
inappropriately, at their comfortably-circumstanced
phrenetics, their faces comically poised for the irrational
and their attempts to cook themselves up into happy
states of imminence; we would justify our presence by
taking drinks and cigarettes; I had a violent argument
with E. L. T. Messens, a Belgian surrealist, in which I
attacked the movement; he accused me of thinking it

necessary to be dirty in order to be an artist; I told him the irrational was rationally contrived, and I observe that Freud said something like this to Dali.

It was at one of these meetings that the poet and critic (Herbert Read) was reading a passage in his war memoirs wherein he said he had an uncomfortable feeling in the presence of a coward; I walked up and went because, I think, I thought I was one; but I took care to see this action as pretentiousness; since then he became my helpful 'patron' in many matters. Surrealism was a revolution, in London, in the sense only of the revolving of the personality. It was a poor echo of the French brilliance, which some of it truly had been—Ernst, Tanguy, Dali, and Eluard; their paintings were often appalling messes of viscosity and heavy ambiguity, devoid of the lightness, the lyricism and freedom and conciseness of their French counterparts: I liked Wyndham Lewis's attacks on the movement.

Elsewhere I met *Poetry and the People*, a communist publication prematurely exhibiting social-realism, near to Baptist hymning and frustrated by a narrow-principled hostility, like mine, to the middle-classes who, it's too often forgotten, are also working-class. I went again to meetings, sold *Daily Workers*, but in a way so abstractedly dutiful that I couldn't persist for more than two weeks.

I employed the term 'dialectical materialism' frequently without knowing what I meant, and understood, indeed, little of communist theory: and my intellectual and petit-bourgeois snobbery kept me clear of working-class affiliations; I was in the way of being, behind a smokescreen of contempt for it, a shrill little literary *entrepreneur*, busily cooking feelings for verse and feeling as wonderful as possible on my small success.

Disparagement of others, especially of the established, played a compensatory part in my self-establishment, so that I was later apt to discountenance all my low assessments of the period poets—unwisely, I think. All the time, though, I felt myself compelled into a polite amiability in manners that meant very little to me, and over which I seemed to have no control: fear must have been the cause. It had a nervous basis; I'd lost my iconoclast's courage; I was still courageous in thought but it had become less bloody. The world had gone bigger and greyer, flatter and more detailedly and impersonally populated: I was seeing existentialist reality.

Now the old life had recommenced, and I routinely trudged for sixpences, from one end of London to the other for doughnuts, tea and Woodbines, rehearsing feverishly my plan of operation over three miles. I painted slobbering pictures with an air of unobserved distinction and sold them to the junkman; my Scotch-Greek girl had left to have her child (my predecessor's) in hospital. I wanted a companion to help me sustain a now enforced privacy, and roamed Fitzrovia in unconscious search.

The engine had run down, it seemed, and life was no longer the exciting drama it had been; all mattered less; the contact with the world had gone; the inertia of my 'intellectualisation' was heavy; I felt confined in a cocoon; in moments that would have led in the old days to excess, I felt the application of unconscious brakes. It became my aim to wear out those brakes, to get back my old naked way of living, which in contrast to the present seemed at least living.

Fitzrovia was a national social garbage centre. But its inhabitants had the sweetness as well as the gameness of humanity gone off. They lived a life of pretence among themselves, and the successful ones pretended also to become outsiders, leaving the district to slander it; I have done this too, but in my case, my leaving had been mainly geographical. In London there were two chief bohemias, the rich and the poor. The rich, or relatively rich, lay round Hampstead and the Bloomsbury the other side of Tottenham Court Road. They were cultured, naturally, and held to scorn by the poor; contacts were infrequent, though they did occur. The poor were recruited from the lower-middle-class, coming of a suburban agony and couched in the clichés of the latter part of the French nineteenth century, with some Wilde. They sometimes settled, cohabited, bred in Fitzrovia, then attaining a slightly higher, if less hopeful status of settled bohemians, acquired the little grace of such, and began to refuse beds to the poorest recruits. In those days, before the war, many painted there. The district almost, never quite, became 'interesting' enough for a residence in it to serve as a *cachet* to the more substantial world of art-patrons and fans. But it never quite achieved its purpose. The uprooted in England, such a small minority, are more uprooted than anywhere else, due to the profundity of English conventions, which can support such a mass of unconventionality merely as a social headdress. The atmosphere was unique; we were like the magic paper flowers that starrily unfold rather chemical loveliness in water. We were babies who prattled ourselves into worlds of great achievements; we looked at and felt about each other amazingly deeply. We were all superbly, and socially surreptitiously pregnant; but never delivered except of disaster; and we watch, sportingly, out for each other's blood. So-and-so's misfired liaison was our only source of security, as was so-and-so's awful picture at the Tate, and the charlatan R.'s memoirs. The charms of the district were those of minimal effort, of paddling in sensations wafted in by the busy proper people surrounding our encampment. A feature before the war was the contact between Fitzrovia and Oxford and Cambridge; it was a minor convention for the misfits at the universities to spread their wings, sometimes on the way down, for a while to stay with us; we clustered round them, of course, like wasps round a jam-pot, and drove them away quickly with our needs as well as our stings. Somewhat, we overdid our parts for their entertainment; but there was always a shop-window element in bohemianism. We felt we might be spotted either as characters or as artists (the distinction was usefully confused) by the powers. But all that is in the past. A diminishing bohemian spirit met half-way an increasingly bohemianised conventionality, notably under the Labour government, whose composition was in part bohemian-inclined. Moreover, after the war, the council classed the district as industrial and it died of the incursion of tailoring sweat-shops; agents probably discouraged such poor rent-payers as artists were wont to be.

Two Canadians I met speaking in the Park, and an American surrealist, all reminded me of the immense disparity between what I knew and the pretensions of what I said. We were all of us rankled beyond repair, maybe, by our social inferiority, by our fringe position on the cultured classes, which our abuse of them couldn't wholly assuage. We felt the right to know so strongly that we dishonestly avoided the realization of our difficulties. We, and the Fitzrovians, were a community expressly made, among other things, to give ourselves legitimacy in the world of culture. We met mutually to inflate, and the tipsiness lasted a while. This makes me now tend to swallow whole the qualities of the class from whom I derived but among whom I was not educated; to defend myself from that without perpetrating old self-inflating deceptions is difficult and perhaps rarely successful. It is not my beliefs that I doubt, or doubted; they come in a long line from childhood, through predispositions, instincts, experiences, and have changed little. But I sense always an inaccuracy in my presentation of them; often, a direct contradiction. A symptom of the distance between expression and conception in me is the naïve pleasure I take in everything I write; its complexity, adroitness, pertinence astounds me—for a few minutes; then, an hour, a day later, it sounds to me peculiarly thin, contrived, as though I'd stolen without the right of heritage the mental manners of my superiors; my modicum of democratic feeling refuses to admit the theft as a crime; so I'm driven to continuing the attempt until the gap is closed between the thought and its expression—not so much the thought as a mangled verbalisation of it which has to be translated into understandable English. (This quality of strain and self-consciousness was common to many writers at this time.) The way out was the private language of many modern poets—a privacy of language, I believe, apart from fashionable aspects, much more due to insufficient culture and education than to any poetical inspiration or heightened individuality; the obscurity, however philistine it may appear to be to say so, appears to me to be marvellously *voulu*, timid of public understanding and coming from the absence of the kind of full culture and understanding which makes for lucidity.

True, elements of language experimentation have their value and necessity; but these lapse into meretricious 'originalities' all too easily. (Dylan Thomas became suffocated by images; the verb disintegrated.)

The obvious symptom of my naïve association of the intellectual with the non-essential worker or parasite was my affectation of the expression and behaviour of such, a sort of witch-doctor with a fraud-killing scowl and façade-shattering penetration. The obvious was my target; I developed a 'port'; studied people under beetling brows, looked fore and aft as at the sinking ship of the state, and wagged my prophetic finger in the face of the obliging simpleton. Later, I performed the world-follied disarray of a great mind, reeling with the vision of chaos. But this mountebankery wasn't my invention; it lay ready-to-wear in the intellectual wardrobe of the times, which today merely has changed for ostentatious discretion and queasy 'ordinariness', as ordinary as my dreams.

I have already spoken of a penchant for looking in the mirror, which I began to develop in adolescence; the extraordinary thing is that the 'faces stayed'; I can trace affectation in manner today directly from some cliché-face in the mirror of twenty-five years ago: and if I thought I was original in something as standardised as the making of Morris cars I'd probably less coldly mention it. I had also an anxiety of not looking normal, partly from masturbation guilt; my faces were mostly expressions of sterling honesty, with some of quizzical and affectionate inquiry, rough nobility, luscious disgust, and homosexual insinuation. Under the disguise I felt and feel still often about five, acting maturity; I've caught so many others at the game, caught them in the early stages at school, so often, indeed that I could take an objective interest in this mass-pre-fabrication of persons—an extension of schools of deportment, mostly English, or Anglican. So, passes are made in proto-identities; identities fornicate to new formulations, are swopped, peddled, bought and sold; that's the courage of the brave new world.

My assumed identities were a preface to meeting some-one whose infantilism or child-likeness was as consider-able as mine, and who sustained it without my vulgar chicaneries and protections.

I think she saw me. She crossed to the pub nearby and I followed: first words are forgotten, first notes of a long piece, of sweet clarity and loud with undertone at once. We returned to the society's rooms, where I was staying.

Faces reminiscent of L.'s are Virginia Woolf's and the 'cello player in John's picture. But hers was lighter and more childish than these; but also (comparing with the 'cellist) less wordily personated; it was as perhaps the youth of Virginia Woolf had been—I've not seen early portraits of her; and certainly Virginia Woolf's writing expresses perfectly my L.'s consciousness of the world. It was as naïve and as purely articulated; had as much insight into the unspoilt delicacy within people, and as great a fear of the mundane overgrowth. She saw human traffic as a procession of moods, as a piece of musical counterpoint in psychic terms; as quadrilles of souls in a still social room with sunshine pouring through the open window, where not a breath of air stirs the brocaded curtain.

But all of her was sculpted in her hands; slim, beauti-ful, brilliantly articulated, seeking and useless. They lay

179

like forlorn deer on the grass. She laughed too often, too quickly, with the happy danger of a child. So she was as private as I; I would attack ferociously that element of privilege in her which had kept her from the sordid vulgarisation I myself had suffered: a miscalculation and lack of understanding that I realised too late. Her privacy was her burden, and she lived in childhood.

It's said by sexual idealists in as many words that good sex is an excess of knowing; the passions, as in a coffee percolator, are boiled up into the mind and drain back intellectually informed; this may be; it may be also that people utterly ignorant of each other, love and mate, and discover perhaps greyly the ashen monster of the uninspected personality, leaping like a jinn from the happy night's box. But the blessing of sex on personality and character of the partner is an undoubted fact; as a key to understanding it has no rival, because every act of cognition and of potential disagreement is accompanied, as on the bass, by a pleasurable memory and tingle; the dry idea soaks in the sexual gravy, and life, understanding, comes: and sexual pleasure exudes an atmosphere of civilisation, as the sea offers rain to parched lands. The desexualised—and, as Lawrence suggests, this includes the sex-worshippers—are commonly intellectually inferior to the rest, being dehydrated; their analysis becomes destructive; they cerebrate in a desert. That puritanism is barbarism need no longer be doubted; I include in puritanism, of course, the species of debauchery which is insatiable.

My social vice has been passivity, and my sexual vice was adapted accordingly—taking the reverse of the Freudian view. I continued the abstractedly fluent social commerce I'd acquired with women since I'd left hospital, keeping them thus at a distance. I would chatter myself into 'spirituality' and in behaving my way out of it I raised women to the Virgin Mary's safe eminence, like many Americans and decent people generally; there, she can only be earthed again by mud-spattering: worshippers of women are all desecrators of them. I chattered myself into winsome childishness, building up my mother before me and in the resultant dissatisfaction I abused her.

With L. the battle was joined; she wanted normal sexual relations as something morally desirable as well as romantically wonderful; but she was incapable of being satisfied, by the many men also who preceded me. Sexually she liked toughs; she regarded, like many of her class and background, orgasm as the fruit of affectionate violence; she later developed overt masochism. She had wonderful intellectual conceptions of sexual apotheosis, the despair of her lovers. She was reduced to becoming the impotent pilgrim of the orgasm, and an extraordinary example of socio-experiential retribution against 'over-spiritualisation'.

CHAPTER ELEVEN

L s father had been a successful lawyer in Scotland. Quite rich in inheritance, he'd been vague about money and left the family fortune somewhat depleted; its foundation was tweed manufacture. The mother was partly Irish, a beauty; the father, his photograph indicated, had the dreaminess of L., her far-focused eyes, her thin level eyebrows, an air of questioning affection; a body surrounded, its pose told one, by alien things, whose references of association went back in time instead of being socially around; he was partly Franco-Jewish (connected with a banking family) and was not unlike the poet Rilke. The mother was an ardent-eyed beauty; something, perhaps, for the father to be evasive to. L. had been exceptionally devoted to both parents but particularly to her father; he died when she was seven, the mother when she was twelve. So L. was brought up by aunts in a large country house, somewhat strictly, in the intention of her continuing the social elevation of the family by marrying into the 'county'; but she wished to study, and went to Newnham. There she read History and English, had been, an inquiring psychiatrist friend told me, 'brilliant'; but had contracted an interest in love-living and, in the throes of an affair more interesting than the rest, and having gradually ceased studying, had (I think, but am not certain) been sent down: in any case, it was without a degree that she came to London with a thirst for life, which she began to take bottled in the brewery of it, Fitzrovia, arriving there by way of the cleaner Bloomsbury. There was, as I've said, a connection between Fitzrovia and the universities in the 'thirties, in the days when the arts were still somewhat 'flowers of evil' and before *la boheme* had quite developed into a flat joke.

In the cleaner Bloomsbury L. had kept open house for the brilliant indigents around. She was always enamoured of other people's predatoriness, confusing it possibly with virility (on their advice); she offered, I remember, money and goods with a sense of guilt in their possession, and an air of having been shrived by losing them to others; her ordinary sense of property was nil. (The increase in cynical 'realism' about money since the war is so marked that people of another world are hard to imagine; they compare with our contemporaries as the open fields to the prison yard, wherein maniacs trudge with the sense of liberty; the lower-middle-class contribution to ethics— 'self-respect'—is here with us. That self which is thus respected had better cling to its mysteriously enfolding shrouds.) She became the local 'catch' of course; yet those who caught never stayed for long, because she depressed them with the intensity of her desire, her worship which confused them, probably, with a sense of their inadequacy. I drank myself out of a similar feeling.

However, her sense of some good quality in men, was, I think, infallible—what the quality was I'm not sure. It wasn't talent or decency or honesty; it was something like homeliness, gentleness once the tough trimmings were doffed, pathos too, perhaps. She loved to shield, had incorruptible loyalty, and though she did not assess subtly what was unjust—to her it was largely the hurting of anyone by the authorities—yet she had a passionate detestation of what she considered to be so; but it's foolish, certainly, to refuse to call this wisdom. Only it wasn't practicable—the poorest criticism of it. Yes, this was her supreme quality, which I would expect to find hard to make credible; it was an unsentimental (for its issues were immediately practical activities of succour from her) wisdom of belief in the goodness of her friends and loves, a sense of a common heart with them. The wisdom was visible in her eyes,—a wisdom imperturbably serene, which only her small forehead expressed. The reflex to help those in trouble was not only immediate but recklessly large; there too lay her social 'old-fashionedness', remote from the Welfare State. She was personal in all her responses, never referred to principles or institutions as agents or causes of relief. She had a wild violence when on these errands of help, could be stopped only with physical force; was completely fearless both of consequences and obstacles: but also very unskilful in their overcoming. Had her brain been in keeping with her heart and her soul—less romantically absorbed—she would have been what we call 'a great woman', of the order of Florence Nightingale or, more exactly, as we think of Jeanne D'Arc. She's the most wasted woman, or person I know.

I knew she had some money when I saw her, but cannot remember thinking so, because, largely, my mother also, in my most vivid and earliest memory, had been of her 'class', which made her the more familiar to me. Strange that I hungered for one of my mother's class—with no 'snobbery', but as for one who spoke my emotional language. The language of my guardian had never been properly assimilated by me; it seemed semiarticulacy, a matter of crooked grunts and groans, though I made a faith of finding such inarticulacy more poetic than the other. Her having money, I said, made her also more familiar; and by association dovetailed into my parasitic nature, largely formed by a mother whose magical appearances meant the atmosphere rather than the fact of 'luxury'. My ease with L. was marvellous; and it wasn't guile, my parasitism—perhaps it rarely is. The strange thing with me was that I was willing, at times, to take the pride of its having been guileful, swaggeringly; but I didn't do it well. I hadn't enough sense of the necessity of independence. Though I scorned employment, it was a matter of the believing the grapes to be sour, for I felt unfit; further the freedom of being out of it was meat and drink. Though I've had to change since, it took a long time before I found the freedom delusory. Though I would have known more about my fellow-men's hearts and hidden decency by taking a job, I would have known less of their minds and manners. (I am now repairing the former—enforcedly.)

We spent several nights of asexual intercourse in the studio, and then moved next door to a friend's and found a convenient source of 'spiritual' food there, in a bottle of benzedrine. We tangled so in our branches that our roots were forgotten. We bathed in all the moods of love of the day, in Tzigane records, black coffee, wine; I seized all the cerebration the asexuality provided for the blowing of egotistical fanfares. I babbled as never before, vomited my life before her, for her, as though for her to take away, to rid me of it forever, to live in her thereafter. I seemed to be struck by the incredible misery to date, of its mean inhibitions, its emotional starvation. I talked to her twice a day for five years, and she listened. The world went, seas spread, and I embarked into the little boat of the moment, verbalising all my dingy landlife. 'Myself' became endless rolls unfolding of scintillating silk, running through my fingers and filling the world; since we separated this textile has been methodically diminished, and I expect a pocket-handkerchief like anyone else's when all's done. She would minister to me, bring me coffee, cigarettes, wonder if I was comfortable, cold or hot or hungry: this was the intensity of consideration that had appalled her previous loves. Evidently I could 'do' with it. But I soon twisted it into a tribute to my merits; and this she never saw. I scrambled out of the poverty of this into autocratic bad-temper.

We soon moved into a flat in the same street, where the local parasites descended in thicker swarms; I felt, here, less my love than my kingdom threatened, though I was ordinarily jealous enough. I remembered how easily she'd wandered to me, as a sense of the equal possibility of her wandering away. I became more mercenary, and tried to hide my love of new clothes and interesting food and drink and the huge soft bed of security.

I tried to separate L. from our friends of the district. I had also attempted to convert her, on an understanding whose limitations were fuel for fanaticism of a safe kind, to communist views. We'd attended meetings, she contributing at my bidding to party funds, but nothing very much came of it for us. She was far braver than I, needless to say; I think my evasive attitude was more effective than my oratorical fire in influencing her not to become too involved.

As was normal for my times, I wanted to 'live', which meant to be drunk, before the generally expected deluge. I wanted also to see France, the country of my childhood,

and my soul's 'island': I expected to become as I'd been
and see what I'd seen there in my childhood—most of all
the unthinking fluency, my being organised into a local-
ity and people unknown to me since. My remembered
maman, too, beckoned me. I was escaping as well the
frightening embarrassments of having begun to act on
my communist convictions—I'd been to the Bermondsey
affair, and was thoroughly scared. I wanted to leave
everything of 'grown-up' civic consciousness forever, or
until the debacle rather which would, like icy water,
almost killingly cure me to maturity. Further I'd been in
a state of sometimes shameful invalidism, increasedly
nervous and erratic, since I'd left the hospital: the
'abstract', induced compulsion to control which had been
its gift to me was curiously irritating, like a grip from a
policeman. It exacerbated what I'd always had much of,
individualistic anarchism. I thought I could leave that too,
with its accompaniment of deficiency in confidence and
worse, with its feeling of being uprooted from emotional
sources (which hasn't gone yet, and which has made the
association of feeling with drunkenness so strong). I'd
begun to jeer at all expressions of emotion. While I had
taken no more risks, I was building up the divinity of
risks: the raising of the temple of my little chaos meant
the sinking of this financial raft; and I had no more
thought—care of, consideration of—money than when
I'd had none. Already I was beginning to throw it away,
as delicious dirt. Furthermore I'd been taught by my
mother to hate England and the English—in a litany—
and the seeking for childhood and obedience to her
precepts went together. I regarded their majestic un-
emotionalism as a cunning providence of shock-absorbers
and a calculation for profit: I seemed to see the withered

seed of a natural heart in the plump growth of that equivocal 'decency' so right for the market. To impassion an Englishman was to disintegrate him: the signs of this were the disgusting disembowelments that the orthodox strains conditioned and allowed in the bohemian district. Their ultra-fashionable attitude to art, also, repelled me, depressed me, made me philistine; they seemed lacking in any native happiness of making— facsimiles of this abounded in the craft-art faiths. One dared not really 'down' into oneself for the making of things—verse or what not—because one was—as simple as I—compelled into a ravishing and killing amazement at one's 'depth' gathered merely from hearsay. The intrinsic was astounding, instead of normal. Freakishness was *de rigueur*, even as morose anti-freakishness. The thing, the sometimes quiet, sometimes integrally rhapsodic real thing was untouchable—by admiration. All was virginal mentation of the creative act (such a phrase!). Even at school I couldn't move without being remarkably funny. This might be I don't know what—perhaps Irish homeliness, such as lay so obviously behind Wilde's sheen. The people laughed at the particular and practical combined—at the art as science: it had to be inexact, either spectacularly or mystically. Art was inexactitude. That was forced on me very early, provoking wooden or brutal 'fundamentalism', forcing one to craft in lieu of science-art. All these made enough to leave 'forever'.

I soon left 'forever'. I was in too much of a hurry to go, almost, to Mother, to France, to wait for L. who had some emotional parcels to tie up. So I went alone, and arriving at Dieppe at once observed that my Anglican raiment and my technical and unreal maturity with its apish ways had stuck. Just a small emotional replica of a

child stayed in my stomach; and its thirst to keep alive
was at once enormous: the more it drank the temporarily
larger it grew, till in high intoxication it and I were one;
and in the hangover, correspondingly wizened and dead
it lay, while I looked at the mapped and ashen world. I
drank as a cynic to become drunk as a child. I then began
to believe more seriously in the universal wisdom of
children, and when later I read the *Idiot* knew at what,
minus the Christian idiom, I'd aimed.

I stayed in a small hotel in Montparnasse, and the only
pleasure I remember was the accompanying music from
the film *Peter the Great* at the contiguous cinema, and,
a little more chilling, meeting M. Kogan, a good sculptor
and most kindly man (later dying in a German concentration camp). He indeed looked at me as one who was the
epitome of the fundamental law that says: One must
mature. I saw it in his eyes as a man's greatest sacrifice,
his experience of greatest agony, without which nothing
could be done. But it merely frightened me; I think it
was prophetic. I've seen this in a few of the best men I've
seen—distinguishable from the rather sentimental glow
of one who matured in attitude only. It is the sacrifice
most abhorred of 'romantic' poets: and one feels about
it, of course, that one will lose 'all one has' which in
England is inextricably involved in arrested development; and demanded of art as inexactitude. M. Kogan
made me feel remarkably thin; all these moments of
thinness added their layer of vulgar evasion on to me. I
felt a spiritual mannikin.

CHAPTER TWELVE

With L. I at first developed wonderfully a technique induced by minor parasitic acts: that of ignoring my financial needs at one moment, doubly emphasising them the next; I would be vague at the proposition, and then, by sleight of hand, take what I wanted: would not accept on request. I began constantly and diffidently to say no before accepting; this had quite deep effects, so that when others were at the receiving end, and even now when I'm shopping, I can't concentrate at the moment of transaction, but swear meanly afterwards at my inevitable loss. I shuddered at all mention of money; looked at L. with implied difficulty in hiding a psychic distaste at her rentier status; I think she believed the accusation genuine. But I was happy as a child materially; and a vacancy of some kind of unemployment built itself up in me like a cancer. Even as the train moved out of Victoria all seemed to be *too* well, like an unhealthy appetite. I was to withdraw from people through money as much as I had through other matters, and more speedily and more cruelly; I was unplugged from the mains in a very short time.

Paris had plenty of London's bohemia round Montparnasse at this time; the atmosphere was the traditional one of hard-worked sin, talked about with fanatically puritan expressions, or as doctors might speak of a desperate operation. But having side-tracked this issue so far

I wasn't in a position to make a good assessment, and was deeply embarrassed. One tediously flamboyant character from London said he'd had five women at the brothel with the air of having cut five trees down in the forest and returned breathless from the task. I didn't know whether this was great or not, but saw that it was held deserving of a laugh. Standards of virility, having something in common with those of cricket, hadn't ever worried me; they were generally infused with the English curiously bitten emissions, where a fist's hit has something of a handshake and vice versa. My conceits were more 'intellectual', or worse.

To remove ourselves from what amounted to an erotic 'theatre workshop Paris' we moved into a sentimental-seeming little street called that 'of the Swallows', into a little hotel hidden away. Here we found intimacy again for a while; the lack of the physical was now beginning to be exacerbated by the intensity of the rest. I wanted to be with her but not to be: to know that she was there but to have to sustain the weight of her presence, which was the weight of her sexual absence from me. I felt vicious and apologetic, and began to concentrate on the monetary aspect of our relationship. I began to buy things in great excitement, especially gramophone records and wine. A dreadful unreality seized me as a licensed purchaser; I was becoming as abstracted from my surroundings as I was from myself. I was becoming thoroughly 'disengaged': the preceding 'engagement' having been hard, I hadn't enough to regret. To be accepted as a conventional, legal customer of things was like being in a film which previously I'd only seen. The performance was continuous; I felt a giggly humour in the solemnity of the purchaser's world, and experimented in 'taste';

all this was treated so seriously by so 'grown-up' shop-keepers that I was nearly alarmed into thinking it a very serious matter myself. I became weighty with purchase, and to consider my soul with the complacent connois-seurship of the contemporary poets. This was a recur-rence of my childhood farces of finding devils under floors and being in communication with God. With a despairful cynicism looking for the 'calling of its bluff' which I nevertheless made sure of not meeting I frowned critically at all the world, and was steadily eating up that capital of community, what was available of it, the loss of which was to make things so hard later, when the economic ego had gone.

I was increasingly frightened and guilty before the working-classes, especially waiters, whom I over-tipped 'madly'. L. walked by my side never-ceasing in her disciple's adoration, accepting everything I said to the point of my annoyance at such self-compromise—which, nevertheless, was never exploited by her, then or after.

We moved south after a month or so to Sanary, near Toulon, and there stayed first in a hotel and then in a studio overlooking the bay. Here my oratory of the second bottle became fully developed, in two daily sessions; I imagine I was attempting to talk away my life, since that had become so inactive, so merely technical. Everything but talk bored me, and everything to do with other people. Here L. frequently betrayed me by taking an interest in them, at which I was always deeply indignant. I could see sometimes an irony in the seas' little waves purling towards me, in all movements of nature, and more in those of people. Nothing they said justified this feeling, but I felt I was becoming a figure of fun to man and nature. I talked all the more to validate myself and my

intellectual enterprise. My emergent theme was the
approaching deluge, to which I looked forward eagerly,
feeling that I was saving up for a combined destruction
and baptism. I was very eager to get rid of all L.'s money
which, I said with some truth, kept us from other people;
for thought I sneered at their manner I worshipped
something I imagined to be their matter. Money was a
raft and humanity the sea, and I said we must sink to be
saved. The practice of my preaching was sardonically
enjoyable. I persuaded her to sell shares continually; her
passivity was increasing; she never told me what she
thought of me in those days. I think our mutual childishness made this impossible. I felt very grown-up when I
bought a car, and could watch with awed amazement the
serious attentions gravely given the thing by garagists, as
though my journeys were necessary. I raced up and down
the coast imitating some film-star figure on desperate
errands of emotion, or a romantic poet; round the corner,
at the destination, it had become a convention to expect
the enlightenment and the bliss; movement became
continuous. Tedious were the days L. liked, of going to
the bay and bathing. Whenever we were still and alone
together there came a moment of strangeness when I
babbled, and then one of my infancy, when I ceased and
rested by her side. I missed that part of my intelligence
grafted to my hunger and indigence; there seemed no
need to do anything. I missed my appetites in their
stupefying satisfaction; sex-starvation was practically
used to keep the habitual anxiety and its cultural cosmetic in process of manufacture, and to smother the
sense of chronic unemployment. I prevented the communication I secretly desired with her, by biting off
everything she said or did to refute it; I must have been

frightened of a possible perception on her part of my fondness for the fleshpots. But actually she took it as very normal, that I should eat and drink as much as possible; she did so herself to a lesser extent, loving food as people. I fixed firmly upon her the guilt of having money and the disgrace of not letting me have all of it, at once, to throw away; some dizzy paradise of maximum expenditure dawned upon me, when one became an abstract god, walking with long pelican legs upon a spread of human emotions which all came from money, the desire for and the lack of it.

I wanted her to leave me alone, and as ever, without my telling her—another curious and more tragic instance of this happened later—she obliged by having an emotional call to London. She'd been unreciprocatedly in love (of the flesh) with a young handsome man there before I'd met her. She now went to see him to see if a union was possible. I then went off, on her departure, to the local brothel, finally accepting her as too near—and, I think, too 'good'—for a sexual partner. At the brothel I achieved a rudimentary normality which was to take me much longer to acquire properly. I developed a physical exhibitionism which I could still trace in a violent wish to communicate, and which drove me later back to writing, to the need to puzzle out a case-history. For I was never unwilling, but eager always, for a good diagnosis without personal bias, but never found it. Never finding it made the search for it and the trafficking in vague approximations a later teatime luxury. I found some temporary stability by turning over in the car down an incline; I enjoyed for a while the enforced sobriety, went through rituals of modesty till the shock was over, and recommenced.

194

L. returned with two little communist friends from London, I meeting her at Boulogne. The healthy pleasure of these depressed and discountenanced me; I was near enough to a starveling's appreciation—in my case greed—to shudder at the base communion implied, and became very unpleasant in the attempt to appear an *habitué* of good living.

The man, of weaker principles than his wife, didn't discourage my intoxicated eccentricities, but his wife became shrewish, for which I admired her. I went to see Madame Tillieux, and couldn't turn her looking after me into a commercial transaction by paying her the long outstanding debt. She looked at me as at a 'gentleman', which added to my 'darkness'; Berthe attempted the old communion, for which I'd become unfit; Pierrot was gentle and remote; Jeannette, whom I saw later, alone was equal to the occasion, thus verifying my earlier opinion of her. Apart from L. I couldn't now like those who liked me, because when I was sober my opinion was otherwise. A gallery of critics of various calibres was forming in my mental apartment: proletarians, shopkeepers, wise people, sensitive people, striving people; only when the bailiffs came in was I to succumb to their strictures. But I hurried to bring the bailiffs in. Returning to Sanary I stopped short of a fight with the oriental impresario who arrived at my invitation; he still hung around L. Then the American surrealist came, a great dirty urban creature absolutely immune to sunshine and sea and French graces, all of which heavily amused him. He came like the customer, and would return with what kind of loot I cannot imagine.

We went off to Greece, through Italy. In Athens I saw Tino Rossi and the Parthenon. I benefited from the dignity of a peasant defecating on a hillside in bright light when I asked him the way back to town.

I wanted to go farther east, but L. was unwilling and we returned to France. The gathering war news limbered up the scraps of identity remaining under the glad rags of its parody. I was too frightened of the prospect to know my fear; it was an approaching coffin of ice dawdling with crazy inevitability my way. Sipping my Dubonnet in the café I remember the waffling frivolity of the paper's turning leaves, the safe patter of feet in front, the peaceful palms and tinkling sea, like a natural boudoir one has a minute more to be in before the police arrive. I scorched myself on the cliffs outside the little town, by Mr. Huxley's old villa, gazed at the sea below with contentions of murder in my heart: they, it was clear as daylight, would soon 'get me', of which I was terrified; but I was grateful for the fear. The time had come that it was better to be communalised by imprisonment than have a day more of cancerous 'freedom'. L. again returned to London; she wanted us to go to America, but I refused; neither east, then, nor west, but back to the national gaol. I had a final debauch in the brothels, and in the middle of it had a charming shopping expedition with two of the girls. We chose stuffs for a dress; a man there said it was war, and I was baffled how to return his tragic look. As ever, unable to contribute to a common emotion, I at length seemed beginning to learn how to do the first stages—by refraining from wagging an artificial expression of sympathy, and by waiting for perception.

I then self-consciously headed north in the caravan of escaping or repatriating Englishmen, on a journey that was, though I didn't know it, necessary. Cars the opposite way in the famous stream chilled me slightly. I arrived at Boulogne, but had to move on to Calais to take the car over. I remained drunk on board, dreading the revelation in sobriety of the heart's contraction at the prospect of Britain.

I drove from Dover to a block of flats, settled myself in a haze of unlocation, feeling the familiar damp hands of English climate, the webs of English politeness and discretion on tap, the slowness of deep-drawn emotion. The failure of my journey abroad relegated nostalgia for the past from emotion to sentimentality, at which I played as often as possible. I wasn't cured, but warned off the premises.

For some days I was unable to find L., and panicked at an emptying bourse; I found her and loved with equivocal relief; it seemed better to reiterate my filial dependence than in a lust of self-reproach to picture a plain cynicism.

Back in London, class pressures, to which my tour of several had always made me susceptible, drove me into the aristocratic-smeared *déclassé* middle, which was basically anarchistic, demanding, defensive, separatist. There was no essential change from my bohemian days: this thing was the moneyed flower of that, and I found the arguments against bohemianism only in the respectable version of it—it had been too necessitous much to be questioned before.

Our whims were become of the greatest importance to us; we chose people for their ears and their perfection of expressed friendship, food and wine similarly, and places to live in. L. loved to laugh with a freedom I'll envy all my life at the spectacle of anyone wanting to cheat her; he was then a cute mannikin, an endearingly so human little fox-terrier up to his specific tricks and expressor, really, of the most crookedly reached affection in the world. Indeed, I believe there is love of the exploited in the exploiter: the kind of love which was evidenced in what I was told of—one soldier battering another on the ground with his bayonet and crying with pity for him, or of the comradeship another felt in the war for the unknown men he was shooting at, which no doubt increased as his gunsight approached the vital spot of his affection's object. Man loves man, and he turns his back on him lovingly to circle round and stick a knife in him: not cynicism, but the physics of a mad system of humanity.

People confused us out of our orientation whenever we saw too much of them. We would give birth to laughter through our mutual observations of the incredibly serious deportment of people about their appetites and appearance and self-conception; every man was a stalwart château in which there was a rapid opening of windows, drawing of curtains, wagging of drawbridges to the degree of phenomenal care and self-concern; every man a country, with the most careful legislation for behaviour. 'Why?' we always asked, and never got the answer: which is dim, dingy and terrible.

But I didn't notice that what we laughed at was much of ourselves.

CHAPTER THIRTEEN

The block of flats we were lodged in was pointedly hideous, for the benefit of the lower group of the transiently prosperous; they demand, it seemed, acids in their colours, a near-kick in their food, an altogether off-colour existence—maybe the first stage beyond 'reality'; a cheesy *chinoiserie*, a heavy subservience from staff to new emergents from unknown depths. The ugliness fed my growing hysteria. Falling became my faith; I thought reality was on the floor, not above it. In verse form I'd already done this (in reaction to the sense of elevation too abstractly produced by the hospital) in the following terms:

> *Down the shute whose sides*
> *are black with feathers squealing with the*
> *   fright of my dream*
> *goes the bundled heart*
> *to a white bulb blooming on the bottom*
>
> *gather in your robes*
> *streaming like hair in the bitter drafts*
> *rolling deliriously in the flight of your fall*
> *bind your limbs to you be a helpless thing*
> *falling to this bulb and fundamental*
>
> *laughing like the spilling of wine*
> *bathing in my shrieking skin I impinge upon*
> *the air down to the glowing light's node.*

Apart from vogue-ery the meaning is clear enough; erotic passivity was, I anti-freudianly think, a corollary, or re-agent. 'Fundamental' meant 'low', associated with decadence. All elevation was into a sky of lies aerially inhabited by middle-class angels.

Tchaikovsky filled the room at this time, for the purpose of our relishing misery, and Rina Ketty singing *J'Attendrai*, Bloch for violin, and Kreisler's *Beethoven Violin Sonata*, and the *Kreutzer*, the *Apassionata;* on great days the *Ninth*; the French *Six*, and Stravinsky for hangovers. I surfeited on music, leading the better part of my life in it. I drank much more, and was at one with De Quincey, and Heine in Cheapside.

Being terrified of the expected air-raids I arranged a tour north with L. and the wife of a friend, a negress, with whom I ogled endlessly but never slept, having never been really promiscuous. There the clean sheet of Scotland made me most depressed; life here was approached only with tools, knives and forks, scalpels; decency was in a white apoplexy; words smelt of toothpaste. The moral coldness was frightening. We hurried to the relative south again, where we could at least become lukewarm. We moved soon to a flat in Mecklenburg Square, where the dreary routines of alcohol, fringe-life of the despised culture groups, epileptic exhibitionism, willed misanthropy, and sentimental prostration before the working-class continued. Here I bought musical instruments, a saxophone, guitar, piano and percussion set, and pummelled away on everything. I was obsessed with my 'genius', which I treated as a hot liquor to be expectorated on the world to its advantage. I abhorred all thought of craft, believed equivocally in surrealist purgation. I always tried to write, but the words slowly streamed together and rolled up in a ball of pregnant inarticulacy. I was tiring of the whole affair; and we both, now, wanted to go into the country, so we rented a house on Box Hill: the first recapitulation having failed, I embarked on the second and lesser. Here, to be thorough, I bought Meccano sets and Hornby trains, like Field-Marshal Goering, and played quite a bit with them. I cooked meats in alcohol, and my inside too, and consistently avoided all sobriety. I yearned more than ever for the end, but it ironically was approaching in a dismaying regulation.

We now became more articulate with each other, inventing a baby language which could express what we most wanted. A man, for instance, was an 'isage', who most *is*, ornamentally, as a contrivance. Actions, in their, to us, cardboard splendour, were 'uptonesses' formed by our being, or not being, 'up to' them. Here the battle against actualities and damp memories was stiffer; drink began to fail to work, and more ill-health was called for: naïvely I wasn't too keen on this, revealing a specious lack of involvement in my goings-on.

But the mood of war-London, especially of left-wing hangers-on before Russian intervention, was conducive to all this; an abdication in favour of omnipotent history prevailed, and the left played the right luxury game of debauchery and drunkenness—or the circle I knew, of writers and painters, did. To be truthful, I was shocked at their behaving almost as stupidly as I, but assumed it must be a part of maturity, and had an easier conscience.

One day I drove in my new, larger car to my guardian's hut, and took him out for a drink. He was dismayed at my 'maturity', however, and sad at the gone association. He was reserved, implicitly critical. I gave him up again.

Turning up at the recruiting office I was rejected on health grounds; delivered from an ordeal into a secret disappointment and a surface rapture. Box Hill being as unrecapturable as France, we returned to London and took separate apartments, I in Fleet Street and L. in Chancery Lane. The raids had begun, and I was too frightened even to realise the danger to the extent of using shelters. But I felt more 'communalised': shared danger had its vitality. I once used the shelter under our block in Fleet Street and I remember losing all sense of ego, feeling quite one with the rest when the bomb by its scream seemed to be coming on us; I didn't yet know of less desperate means of communication. But as salvation from ourselves the war, as any other 'set piece', failed completely to save us from 'ourselves': it had the opposite effect. What precisely the community was in war-time was more clearly revealed than in peace-time. What is essential in a community is a gearing of self-interest to collective interest; since it lacked this its demands in emergencies was a theatrical performance of unity, of patriotic bonds, that was absolutely missing in fact. There developed an awesomely embarrassing *manner* of comradeship, of almost theatrical equality between self-conscious public service workers, for instance, and their social superiors; both sides engaged in a charade of being together that owed its continued existence—it held that flawlessly—to an immense fund of social sentimentality; and this sentimentality, interestingly, was produced by the lack of genuine unity it concealed. The falsity of the 'fineness' of the broadcast material, for instance, is proven in its moribundity, as deep, perhaps, as the Anglo-French *entente*. With the suspension of immediate competition in many of its visible forms came also the suspension of a competitive struggle to be resumed; this stood in an analogous position to the reality as religion to life. I remember myself when participating in the mime ritual becoming breathless, exhausted, as I had been in church in childhood; this 'upper' exhaustion was the fruit of imitation community and held together by the imitation Christian ethos which Lawrence had so acutely seen working in sex relations, and which he called the 'white consciousness'.

It was largely this background that made the raids so terrifying to me; unable to join in the charade of anglican unity I felt dead before the event. Personal life in an artificially communal one was gingered up to fantastic hysterias: the borough most exempt from it in war-time, Chelsea, was the example. Here the fraud was felt, if not seen through—a penetration dangerous to an unequal intelligence. This fake community was a fine basis to social-democratic demagogy, and could be one to something worse: let's not forget the cricketing atmosphere in our relations with the Germans, which is being developed into their approaching new innings. L. was saved from destruction one night by my telling her not to go home—her flat was blown up in the night. She moved to a block farther off, living with a left-wing friend who has since retired from the political fray. I was most indignant, giving her the orthodox slap in the face demanded of a mannikin steadily diminishing in a sense of perspective; and continued my sample of prostitutes. At the same time I founded with Doon a magazine for non-professional writers who wrote mostly about their work; it did well until I ran out of money. Our 'proletarianisation' was fearfully in sight—we thought it was that, continuing to substitute the metaphysical transmutation of souls for the alteration of economic circumstances; poverty, actually, the next time, was to initiate a period of the most crimped conformism for me. The left-wing lover eventually went and for economy I closed the magazine and the flat and moved into her new place.

It was now that she began to show symptoms of mental unbalance, which I hardly viewed as such, partly because of my own eccentricity and partly because of the force of logic (of a symbolical character) common to mental unbalance. She complained of Indians staring at her with wicked intent, and frequently crossed the road; she would jump off buses in motion because she thought the driver was taking her into ambush (the kind of thing I'd played at in my early childhood); and once or twice she disappeared for two days or more and returned dusty and bedraggled, as though she'd slept in the park. Her habit of 'over-understanding' me—a parody and development from the 'depth' conversations common to the period immediately before—made communication hopelessly involved with her. The thing that most frightened me was to see her almost deliberately walk into a lamp-post and not stop until her nose had been badly banged, and her slow realisation of the pain—after an interval in which pain had been 'comically' quite a different sensation to her. She had moments of rapt enthusiasm for simple, sensible projects—such as learning photography, for instance: and would then stop going to the school. This was also my way; but in others I assumed it meant more, for I'd always allowed myself the largest licence in erratic behaviour: my form of 'madness' was to be 'comic' respectability. Obscenity, also, from the scratch beginning of little boys' drawings, was becoming an incongruous trait in her; she had succumbed to the popular 'humour' of sex, knowingly: this was quite irrelevant in her, and boded ill. The left-wing lover had been brutal, and her craving for shock increased. She liked to wander with fine-cut independence of appearance in raids on the streets, shrapnel falling round her. Her fearlessness was frighteningly, to me, a wooing of disaster, the demon lover.

My own unbalance was equally developing, perhaps; I made the most complex mental exploitation of the abstract state of 'hangovers', achieving seeming combination of objects and thought, leading to paranoiac delusions. But I had (perhaps from the hospital) an ability to walk like a cat on hot bricks over my chasms of disaster. I was an able self-nurse; L. was not.

I easily ascribed our troubles to the misery of living in war-time London, painted glowing Millets of rustic life alone together in a little wooden hut I said we could find on Box Hill, and she agreed. We investigated, and bought a little hut in the woods in an encampment. There we took the remainder of our possessions, the remainder of our gramophone records and gramophones, some Chinese drums, books and a suitcase mostly full of *pâté de foie gras*, most of which was eaten by a cat we acquired. We were down to the last few hundreds, and the atmosphere was established of being on the brink of what we now more despondently regarded as the proletarian baptism. It was 1943; with noise, alcohol, and years of my talking behind us, the woods and the heath and men began to get their own back, approaching in the phalanxed menace of Eisenstein's Teutons. I descried shadows of dark omen in their experience-ridden faces, a sombre maturity which made me feel hysterically slight and unproved and thin; a dawning self-doubt abetted a furious irritability. I'd wander off to the heath and brood on the melancholy winter scene, watery trees sketched against damp veils of cloud, measurelessly distant horizons studded with melancholy-sweet Valhallas, dampness underfoot, waters of sorrow blown with the dreary eternal information on the ponds, of a continuity, a law, an order (despite the social disorder) which I'd flouted in a vulgar imitation of the disorder. Accusations less moral than intellectually wise poured down upon me, and I grew weak with apology abroad, tyrannical with tattered justice at home. I scented a deep dismayed affection for the heath, the country and world as being an ever present cradle in which I'd done silly things, whose harmonies I'd been deaf to; I felt profoundly improper, more than immoral: for I didn't lose my senses. These harmonies and wisdom with, inevitably, a deal of sentimentalism, I began to discern in the 'stupid' people; its detachment from intelligence was something needing years to accommodate myself to. But Tolstoy was of great help in this, though a wrongly-taken marxism pointed too much against him: reading *War and Peace* again, however, I found aids to continued, more subtle evasion (vulgarised of course by me) in Peter, whose omniscience of sensibility was an attractive pacifist—anarchy and an alternative to a similar intellectual grasp.

I also re-read Rousseau's *Confessions* with a feeling of exquisitely comfortable intimacy, feeling with terrible sorrow what a lost child he'd been. As my degeneracy had been solo, so now my slight mites of regeneration seemed to be. True, I told L. of everything I thought and saw; but I think she'd been immunised against hearing a little more sense by the great deal of nonsense. Anyway, she was becoming what I'd been with her; I was slowly feeling for old roots that must have been before even my early dislocation; such remote ones naturally had to be mystically apprehended, which I did later in Chelsea with my anarchist friend.

Time had to be spun very fine here; cobwebs of it gathered round us. Little insects in their calm cruelty to survive reminded us of depressing things; lost dogs, dead birds, bare trees, our sad drunkard of a landlord—a ravaged ex-officer—all pointed to purgatory. The iron sky held for one long winter, I remember, holding in the damp and the water. L. bored me as the image of one's past mind must; for I had spoken experimentally, if in a dogmatic form, and had never achieved a contribution towards synthesis from her argument. She had been paper for printing, and I'd been only a journalist. She was yesterday's animated news, and I tried to throw her away in the sense of inwardly wanting it. She was too invalid for my invalidism; I was small, and here burdened with a tragedy, which I didn't understand, being remarkably devoid of humanity: its sentimentalities in expression had made me throw the baby out with the bath-water.

It amazes me, now, how tirelessly I hacked away at this humanity, thinking it to death; many of us were thus incredibly cruel on principle, the militant dregs. We were terrified; were playing at revolution against a subtle old monster who didn't turn a hair. Our futility became a mannerism, feyness.

I'd sometimes looked at funny films—Marx Brothers, for example—without laughing, and experienced awful terrors: comedy slipped from the world, and comedy unsustained by laughter is the maddest confusion of tragedy. Laughter is dog against dog: beware of him who aspires to an uncanine reaction—or beware for him, rather. He may go mad. Humane laughter is the holiday of feebleness.

Paradoxes are in the ABC of experience. This one was that, having reached the edge of the bath of baptismal proletarianisation, I should now, as one of the found and saved, go to a Labour Exchange, sign on for a course in inspection, and immediately feel compelled to cultivate a fantastic respectability which led, exactly, to the appearance of a gentleman who fitted oddly in the lower-middle-class surroundings. The complexity of this chain was bewildering, but I managed it for five months. I rose at five in the morning, was cursed with L.'s long-winded attentions to me as of one buckling on knight's armour, would stewing mount my bicycle and ride through the dawn four miles to the station; go through private rigmaroles of insouciant workerliness in the carriage, scanning my face till the proper dim-keen expression was formed, work then for a heart to match, and a twangy nasal personality, arrive at the training centre, doff the whole business to a 'natural' gentility, and in a hurry scurry round to pick up odds and ends of the doffed apparatus: some, not all, seemed demanded. To my astonishment I proved quite competent, but bored stiff after an initially heavy enthusiasm; I looked at L. behind beetling worker's brows, and at the workers with genteel absence.

I became impossible in the hut—very tired, unable to provide emotional fuel, careless of L.'s reactions. She wandered off more frequently and began to tremble. One day she stood on the chair by mine with a wood-chopping axe raised above her head and about to be brought down on mine. I caught her wrist nicely, saved my life with unsuspected enthusiasm, and had coarsely to admit I wanted to live. Wanting to live with no known reason humiliated me, and influenced me into further depravity later: existentialism.

For the next two weeks she tried to approach me with razor-blades and cutlery, a pile of which accumulated under the veranda. I trembled for my wretched life; she said, and I couldn't but agree, that she wanted to kill me because she loved me and she knew we'd never be happy together alive. This was incontrovertible; my desire to live was without logic: or with the mean logic of being content to live alone—and that, I think, was the worst thing I thought. I guided her with great difficulty to the doctor four miles off; when a car approached slowly I said to myself without words, 'run under it'. She did, at once, and lay bloody on the bonnet. Luckily the car had been moving slowly, and she was not much hurt. The doctor arranged for an ambulance days later. At the hospital entrance I spoke my last great speech, of about an hour and a half, to the effect that she owed it to the society which I'd so convincingly vilified to get cured. Strangely, my chief conception of her 'insanity' was of her rudeness. I felt insanity to be impolite, a breach of manners: my own were insufferably rude. She was entered as a voluntary patient.

Part Three

THE END THAT FAILED

CHAPTER FOURTEEN

I left L. at the hospital in a state of manic exaltation and depression. I felt tremendous power and independence at being without her, exactly as it had been leaving my mother; but I was in complete darkness when I sank back into forgetting she'd gone and suddenly realising it; I felt tremendously relieved at being able to be something, so glorious in a prospect which diminished to nothing at a glance; I inhabited at once the fantasia of my solitary grandeur, and yet felt that a ghost was exaltedly trying to crush mountains. I listened, and nothing was there, no one; I had gone with her, and my body careered away like an empty removal van. So long, then, had we been away from the world, from the horrible configurations of its stale 'normality', the gross affectations of its decency, but I remembered with seedy faith that the stuff of all or of much that L. and I had worshipped as 'reality' was inhabited by 'ordinary people' who I could not admit to be other than immeasurably superior to myself in all ways; megalomania had not diminished, but had lost its intellectual supports. I first then experienced a sob involving a contraction of the whole body, becoming a state for a duration, from which no sound emerged, which no tear alleviated. I was horror-struck that she, whom I knew to be of an organic integrity, of a purity unequalled (I use the term purity shamelessly, in spite of its utter untopicality), should be with the mad while they, whom my heart's eye told me were cannibals and idiots, of an unbearable coarseness now that I was exposed to them, that they should be legal, free, accepted, at large. After visits to her during which I would imbibe the perhaps rationally untenable sense of the extraordinary purity of insane people, I would be horrified, shocked, made to tremble at the grossness of the assumption of this normality by wretches who resembled pigs in my perhaps, wild eye. I remember particularly their noises, which it took years for me amiably to distil into conversation, seeming farmyard, racous, brutal beyond belief; the ungainliness, epilepsy of their movements; the horror of their shiny costumes, the shrieking righteousness of their women, the doggy non-existence and sham independence of their men. The bus would reel with this cargo to the station, and I would stupify myself to immobility in the pub before daring to go farther, such was my terrified and trembling indignation at the unbalance of things. It was years before I realised the exquisite completeness of our isolation from 'Society'.

'Myself' being away, which I thought sometimes that I was forever, developed a gruesome facility in social gesticulation. I could tittle and tattle as well as the best; and now and then I felt a curious comfort in odd moments of genuine amiability, with my senses a little eased, in social intercourse; and then I became alarmed at thinking how unpractised I was, what a long way I would have to go to learn, evidently, an unknown language springing from the relative ease with which these monsters held intercourse and lived together. At that point a whole cathedral of pious principles of people-worship would operate, and I would groan sinfully under the weight; which manically, with a toss and a jump, I'd chuck on the roadway, and dart off like an independent madman whose independence tussled might and main with the people in the name of the deification with which I saddled them. If sex were on a lift, and the controls were socially operated—in the widest sense—I'd say society was now, with many a creak of the stiff vehicle, lowering the lift from my brain, where it had become embedded, to its normal level and operation. Each descent was depressing in the extreme to my 'soul of isolation', and warming to an animal in me that had hardly ever lived; the social animal. But more and more I imitated the grandeurs that were the contemporary impression of a gone self (gone with L.), vulgarised, comedied them. I was rushing into an eccentricity I flattered myself was deliberate.

I developed an immense greed; and remembered, with her, how I'd so often longed to be alone with the money she gave me to invest some fantastic sensory heaven with my hungry body; which I'd done before and found, as I was to find now, so bleak, so unreal, so miserable. I returned to the hut which resembled an icily wet black cloak with faces and forms of her enfolded in it. It was possibly the same evening that I began to sell everything, her things and mine, to the local people; I remember conducting an auction, dead drunk, selling my drums and her clothes and eventually the hut as well. Next morning I boarded a bus for London; on the bus I made a proposal of marriage to a stranger on the front seat; she was in the compartment next to mine on the train I moved into, and I heard their shrieks of laughter. Arriving, I rushed away, and bought a prostitute. She was not at all attractive, though a very nice person; in the morning I found I hadn't enough money to pay her, and she said she would wait while I went back to the bank in the country to draw what was left, which I did.

When I left her finally I stood a moment struck by streets becoming a huge tray of nothingness born, I could imagine, by a fate's waiter for disposal of the contents into oblivion. I rushed to the pub to gangrene my soul with the exciting liberty from all burdens the thought gave me, and crawled steadily along to my old haunts. But I was still at the factory, and began to feel, through a desired incompetence of some sort, or an incompatible greatness, to leave it. I wanted my chaos and grandeur back again, without inhibitions. Yet, to my surprise, I began to like being there, in moments of forgetfulness I mean, when the work went smoothly and I chatted, with a nerve-racking prevention of all my agitating exhibitionism, with the others. L.'s trying to kill me still lay below consciousness, and I was pausing, carefully, artfully, in a coma, averagely fluent apparently. I walked very carefully, spoke very carefully yet inserting now and then some shrill opinion to shock and dislocate; I spoke, I remember, affectionately, as to men of a kind I would be leaving. I slowly prevailed upon my acquaintances there that I would soon leave: it became essential, in a few weeks that I should, and the idea occurred to me to decide to try to change the opinion of the recruiting authorities that I was unfit to join the army, because Russia had now joined on the Allied side. I told the office I wished to enlist, and they gave me leave to try, which I did on the telephone; but they would not change their mind, and I wouldn't return to the factory. I sat alone in my terrible room, unliftable objects in the cold everywhere, desolated, horrible looking, many with airs around them of L.'s presence, which I couldn't stand. I packed a suitcase full of various things and sold them to the old junk and art dealer I knew, Mr. Messier. Then I remembered a grand piano and some more musical instruments I'd collected, in storage, and began to hunt for them—I'd lost the address—and in doing so, realised how comforting it was to have a phoney object in life, such as this, when another was missing.

It was during the week or so that I was hunting my piano that I met Ernest in a pub. Ernest, at this time, 'wanted to become a composer'. He was extremely good-looking, very large blue eyes in the sort of blond face that (Hollywood) Russian Imperial Guards might have—delicately large cherry-red lips, palish to healthy pink cheeks, high cheek-bones, square forehead with fair hair *en brosse*, and small stiff moustache; his appearance was not lost on him and he favoured a black mackintosh. We liked each other in a sentimental way at once, and possibly in a quasi-homosexual way, and certainly because we were equal fools about the world, but felt we had more fun than those who were clever in that way. We were rather alike, in fact, but I decided not to see him again, because his eyes induced all my worst follies in me. Then he called on me early one morning; we talked about books and music and I begged him never to call again, but of course he did.

My next new acquaintance was with Meg, a New Zealand reporter who lived in Chelsea; I met her at about the time I traced the piano, and was consequently able to know her until the piano had been dissolved in alcohol. She was a sunny little thing, but uninteresting to me. She thought me 'fantastic', which was beginning to displease me. After Meg, who lasted two weeks with the piano, I found myself penniless—the drums and percussion set had been sold as well. I then got in touch with an editor who was threatening to publish my poems; he advised me to go to a typewriter in Tite Street, Chelsea, and recommended the owner, who became my friend, Anthony de Freysne, son of an Edinburgh industrialist, ostensibly studying criminal law but actually bohemian life.

Anthony rented a large studio on a top floor, all glass roofed which he took pleasure in not blacking out. He was an anarchist, he thought, and liked to live in many ways anyhow, but on a comfortable allowance from home. Anthony was an unusual young man of about twenty-two. His father was immensely rich, a Scottish Knight of great industrial acumen, a benevolent despiser of his employees, and this contempt for the working-classes his son inherited with the qualification that he considered them in possession of more soul than other classes. He had an immense knowledge both of literature and science, but was extraordinarily lazy and asthmatic. He believed in practically nothing, and smoking. He was in love with a Lesbian in Chelsea, and had the peculiar perversion of sleeping with one or even two at a time—I wasn't sure what he did with them. He liked Baudelaire, after whom his vicious little black cat was named, Rimbaud, Egyptian art, Chinese philosophy—Taoism in particular—and the French periodical called, I think, *Crapouillot*; he wrote delicate pornography and very bad poetry. He also painted and encouraged me to. When I first met him we reconnoitred like two cats, a common manner in bohemian circles of the time—soul-sniffing, as it were, of which the next stage was to drop pretty meaning-packed remarks. We both came out pretty well in this but he, being better-informed than I, gave me the kind of self-consciousness which made it requisite to know him better. With him was an aged beauty called Martha, a consumptive and heavy drinker and general liver-around, at the moment living at Anthony's. I stayed the night in the same room as Martha, and she worked somewhat on me, which in the morning didn't feel good to me, though I had to conduct her to a café and round the embankment with the best effort at sparkling-eyed devotion I could muster. In return for this she said I was an artist.

Returning, the new little world was completed by Ernest entering, who proved to be Martha's 'steady', though thirty years intervened. Ernest was well known to both as another liver-around; he seriously entered and seriously sat, and then seriously ate, saying, as usual, very little. This may have been because of the extreme care with which he articulated; I later learned he had graduated in several marked stages from cockney to Oxford; his Oxford had been initiated at St. Paul's School whither he'd been dragged from an elementary school, and developed while potato-lifting in his pacifist encampment. This group, I lumpily considered—a lumpiness to be worked on by Anthony through exploiting my remorse—was unbelievably unreal; I scented pretensions, even in Anthony, to cultural facilities hardly held by any one of them; it did, in fact, reproduce and augment the atmosphere of Fitzrovia on to rather more delicate levels. And this was, as I learned when I moved in to Anthony's studio, how the whole time was spent: the basic element of conversation was the stupidity of 'the others'—all the others, including other art-groups, writers, philistines and the masses generally. But I had graduated to this rather more refined atmosphere, chichily anti-chichi though it was, through the fault, I clearly realised, of having had some money recently and thereby become quite uprooted from what's still to be called 'reality', or society. It was the first round in my re-encountering all I'd despised before; this, the little Tite Street group, was certainly what I'd frowned at, with my Camden Town friends, in the days of my excited indigence, and it drove home to me the element of attachment contempt fosters.

Many vague young men called, whose ethos indeed consisted of sometimes quite hard-working vagueness. Not to know—paramountly, that the war was on, then, that money had to be earned—was the thing; my parasitism was thus condoned and, certainly, had a great deal to do with my sojourn. Yet, I grew to be very fond of Anthony. For one thing, he was the most honest man intellectually I'd met, apart from Doon; he reasoned like the successive falls of a guillotine, flashing the while in eyes and ideas. Then, he was methodically generous, apportioning his income to his followers and to himself carefully, week after week. Then, he was genuinely untidy; he would make a cake, and then go out with the flour all over his expensive suit. His cooking and our diet were extraordinary. He refused to use salt and liked red pepper; his staple food was soya flour, which he boiled with cabbage. Then—an excruciating 'objectivity' that I then much admired, he was capable of eating an immense meal in front of me when he knew I was hungry. Then to my astonishment, lost as I was in admiration of his mental finesse and knowledge, he listened with genuine respect to me. I think he thought I had abilities of some sort, and then he liked my life, sensing its emotional logic at the expense of the other kind which here was thought nothing of. He would call me 'Master Kung', because of my expressing opinions with Mother's infallibility. Further, his taste in painting was good; he favoured Persian painting above all other schools, then Japanese, Chinese, Egyptian, and a few of the French impressionists. Life with him, for the six months I stayed as his guest, was the best I could have done in the rather awful mental state I found myself; he sometimes reminded me of Pierrot and, indeed, we were certainly children. We took immense walks all over London, particularly to the East End, to Chinese restaurants there, to the 'Prospect of Whitby', to the music hall in Poplar High Street, and everything was adventure—what I felt with him I really didn't know, and there was wonder around everywhere; then, I felt secure with him—he was protective, and seemed to think I needed gentleness and affection. His eyes were smoke blue, large, squarish, browed like Mother's—behind ugly steel-rimmed glasses, an excellently level brow, of the essential shape of reason; the most delicate face I've seen in a man, rather like Gerard Philippe's when younger (as he appeared, for instance, in *La Ronde*), with a little moustache that gave him only the most impertinent insignia of masculinity, French not English. I must not omit a certain vulgar envy I had of him for his moderate, and his father's very great, wealth. He always dined at the Ritz with his father; of that relationship I did not, however, think much. It was clear that he admired his father's power in spite of his 'anarchism'.

He loved junk-shops, spending hours in their dusty bowels, and book-shops. I'd say, too, he was the first man who genuinely took the arts more seriously than what was produced through survival-techniques, so different from the art-flaneurs of the surrealist groups, and others I'd met. Indeed, he had no middle-class vulgarity: he was not, of course, middle-class. I wish I could hit on the right account of his strange tastes. True, they had much of strangeness in a rather affected way, but they also had something else. He was more allergic than any man I knew to any kind of violence, expressing himself with furious looks and tense gestures against it; the thought of violence drove him either wild or wonderfully contemptuous; and his tastes in art were conditioned by this. He loved the gentle flowers, the gentle elaborations of oriental painting. He was also foolishly—if that's possible—brave. He delighted in walking abroad in the raids. I being a congenital coward admired this. His treatment of people was fascinating. He would stroke until they purred and then, when they were in what he regarded as a fit state to do battle, would criticise mercilessly their displayed felicities. He treated them as children, as specimens, as lost children come to him for solace.

But—I felt like an old man who had abdicated from the grown-up world; I felt a fraud as well as justifiably a convalescent in taking part in what I had to realise were infantile gestures against something of whose might and intelligence none here had the slightest conception; in a kindergarten made possible within the war-walls, within which the infants' gambols seemed justified because of the cessation of intellectual development war caused. Anthony both bowed to and mocked at me, making me feel an old ruffled father which he sometimes, because of his relationship with his own, liked to burn in effigy. Sometimes, when talk stopped, when we paused in our combined painting, in that large, wilfully 'characteristic' studio, I would become aware of impounding sterility, of forest-stillness when no leaf stirred; then all the props, the French poets, the paintings, the bits of whimsy, seemed hardly to support their own physical forms which our onanistic chatter held together. With my faint depression, depression and faint-feeling, went an urgent, exhausting cultivation of bright personality which felt stale as soon as it emerged to manifestation; a dance of costumes. Moments came when Anthony felt the thinness of the game, and with an anxious look would try to stimulate me to more of my threadbare personalia; it dawned on me that this scruffy personality I was fitting together out of salvaged rags of past wardrobes was alone why I was tolerated. Anthony ended thus: towards the end of my stay with him he met a tough girl, his opposite in every way, daughter of an Indian policeman. I disliked her on sight; she asked for my help in getting Anthony to marry her: she was decided she would do so. I refused, but they were married nevertheless. Three months later both were bombed outside the Swiss pub in old Compton Street. I took over the cat Baudelaire.

After six months I was able to persuade the hospital to release L., who was said to be not cured but made as well as was possible. We took a room in 'The World's End', where Chelsea, hopelessly symbolically, led; it was a semi-basement run by a hard lady who explained her hardness by sniffing up a long moral nose. She was of that ancient order of citizens who morally disapprove of insanity—as I at once knew; L. was frightened of her. Here we commenced our 'hundred days', our dead aftermath. L. had changed vitally under treatment; she spoke very little, her eyes were bigger, her bones more pronounced, a strange courseness invested her flesh, and she listened to me without reaction—not entirely due to the matter of my talk; which had never been the sole cause of her attention. I began our last lap with extreme depression, though alone I'd felt my soul missing; it was a soul with which, I felt, I'd have eventually to dispense.* *Their* world, indeed, had gone closer to me, was at my door: hers was irrevocably closed to it. She sat for hours silently, childishly, poking the fire with her childishly efficient manner, stirring our perpetual stew, rising in sudden rapture to take a dull walk. Flickers of life, like fire-glows on a face, animated her for seconds, and then she relapsed as though feeling a strait-jacket about her. In hospital I'd seen her look so beautiful as to make me cry; they'd put her in a rubber-walled cell for violence, and she was robed in white, her hair long about her, her face in an unbelievable rhapsody; that was the pitch, maybe, to which the 'engine of life' raised her, all for picture and none for life; and from this the decline was dictated.

I took refuge in alternating surliness, when I remembered, and mad optimism, when I forgot. I worked as hard, and not dissimilarly, as 'Our Lady's Tumbler' to amuse her; but the 'thing' within had gone forever; she was trying a rudimentary ABC of normal people's language, hopelessly, her contorted mind spinning behind her words and emerging only from her eyes, in acute shades and glows.

We moved from here to a nearby flat with a kinder landlady, and we let our back room to an old acquaintance of mine, one Mann, a painter who lived by exhibiting his paintings on the pavements in Chelsea. He helped me get a job as fire-watcher in Sloane Square, and I

* Premature.

continued painting and exhibited with him. Mann had little brain in the usual sense, but extreme animal acumen; and, with a healthy animal's sensibilities disliked L., who had no patience for his aesthetic nonsense by which he tried to justify his postcard painting. Then the three of us moved into two studios off the King's Road, and continued as before; I began drinking heavily again. Through lack of a normal sex-life—I discovered a fearful distaste for L. sexually—and through drink, delusions set in. I would sing to L. at the top of my voice in imitation Italian, fascinated by my efforts; I would make funny faces, strut up and down Chaplin fashion, to amuse her; once or twice she laughed, the loveliest gap in the clouds. I see I tried to animate the dead, and that she tried to reach me. L. was dead. I became more unbalanced. Encouraged by my bored acquaintances I began to enact my delusions. I bought a black silk jockey cap and placed this above the trembling body dressed in a black jacket (my last opulence from Savile Row) and corduroys: I purloined a one-stringed violin, I changed my name to Theodore Malice (who, Mann told me, through cunning subservience to authorities in Haiti, obtained financial control of the island) and decided to attempt the stage. Here reality, what I did, and hallucination, what I imagined, fused in a fever of excitement. I practised playing my violin in a scraping sound, like a cat's songs, and sang against it, in a nasal intonation;* I sang 'The Sheik of Araby'. I made cabalistic signs (magic and benzedrine were raging through Chelsea); I began work on an immense revue-play called 'The Public Baby', in which the hero was manufactured

---

* The English police: in this condition I serenaded the prostitutes in Piccadilly; I was moved to the gutter and allowed to continue playing.

for success like a motor-car; I made clay dolls of all the characters and trembled with fear before the peculiar frontier place between reality and deadness they occupied. I then had two auditions, one with Ensa and another with Carol Levis for 'Discoveries', trembling all the while, not knowing if I was acting or not—there was no difference. And into all this stepped a recently discharged mental patient who had been an actor, who fire-watched with me for a week. We argued enormously, in a 'Lear' we were to produce, over who'd be the fool and who the King; and this changed into a symbolical fantasia called Bopeep, and again we rowed over who should be Bo and who Peep.

The buzzbombs were now coming over, and I cowered with a terrifyingly fearless L. in the air-raid shelter in the yard between Mann's studio and mine. Every morning seemed posthumous in our lives, every night an encounter with all approximations to death. I was intent upon finding an apocalyptic vision of enlightenment at night when I closed my eyes; there were doors and doors and corridors leading, in an Egyptian architecture, to an Absolute never reached.

Then Mann suggested we go to Wiltshire with him to his cottage where he thought I would get farmwork; we went, a final bomb landing on the track of the train just before we left the station. In Wiltshire we were popular with Mann's wife, a true, pathetic shrew until the little money L. had got went. I worked for five months on the harvest, secretly, I remember, saving some sort of health, or egoism (they were becoming confused under Mann's influence) to leave L. The more I worked the more vulgarly I began to leave her in spirit. The work ended, I pushed an old man round Salisbury in a bath-chair for two months. That ended. One day, by the Cathedral, something happened, I cannot remember what, but I used the occasion to fly into a rage with L. in which I expressed the whole of my conviction of the futility of being, and of my unwillingness to be with her any more. I left her, to return to London, salving my conscience by going into what I presumed to be the danger of the rockets. I went to our old studio, now sub-let to Ernest. In a few days L. arrived; I refused, panic-stricken, to let her in; she slept in the air-raid shelter. I reached incredible brutality through brute fear; I would not have her by me any more; I valued, evidently, my sanity more than her: and this achievement of mine I came to regard as my damnation allowing me to renounce all care of and interest in myself as a human being; I aped on as an idiot-facsimile. The tremblings and the delusions then were a little better.

From the studio, face-life commenced; I found employment with a bearded inventive genius who, soaked in beer within consular respectability, with shaking hands showed me how to make lampshade frames. I made these in a workshop for six months, and caught myself beginning to exploit, in conversation, my 'colourful' past, which confirmed my self-contempt. The enterprise failed of course, and wandering through Fitzrovia I met Ernest again, who had a room in Maple Street; an unbelievable room. From the door I saw an immense mahogany bedstead with a narrow camp-bed within it, on which the eccentrifying Ernest (he's now an able lamp-lighter) slept in dirty white tennis-trousers. The owner was the old Messier to whom I'd sold paintings, and I worked for him in his shop for a while until I met again the oriental impresario, who told me he definitely would publish my poems, for which I'd done drawings. I sold him the copyright for £30 which—as had happened before—coincided with my meeting a new girl-friend, one Jackie who worked at the Ministry of Information. We moved to the cellar, a very dark one, and here we drank our way through another six months, during a fortnight of which I wielded the lights on variety at the Bedford Theatre. Drink brought back the trembling; I walked along a road as on a tightrope, trying hard to control the trembles; one day on the wall of our cellar, I saw a three-dimensional hermaphroditic figure, in red, green and gold, very like Blake's flying Lucifer. Things reached such a state that, in a phone box, entering trembling, I stopped and the walls of the box began to tremble. I phoned a psychiatrist: 'Shall I,' I said, 'hold on or come to you?' He said 'Hold on'; which I did; I slowly began to feel my way to health—of a kind.

It was now 1945; the war ended. That Christmas I found myself on a pile of coal, having left Jackie, and, as far as I could see, everything and everyone, in the air-raid shelter in the old King's Road studios. At last, in the biting cold on the rocky coal, I relaxed. I am, I thought, on the floor, and cannot go below, or have evidently refused to. I conceived an alphabet of civic life to be learned. Though fluent in decisions mostly merely decorative, I realised, nevertheless, that this one was made of my entire life and self; it was a conclusion. One kind of life had led to this, here alone; it would take another kind to make the first step out of it. Next evening I went to a party and met M., in Fitzrovia; M. is one of the most beautiful people I have met, an Austrian Madonna. She took me in and, though that was a false start, nevertheless started me on a halting road to conformity; wherein I saw, gradually, lay the art of walking orderly without inner conformation to a system and a society which appeals to me no more now than before; the art of ceasing to live a drama in order to see one; the art of discerning in people something greater than their squalid state. Montaigne says, 'The soul does not express itself in grandeur, but in mediocrity'. '... but in mediocrity' is hard to understand.